CHECKOUT GIRL

A Life Behind the Register

CHECKOUT GIRL
A Life Behind the Register

Anna Sam

Translated by Morag Young

STERLING

New York / London
www.sterlingpublishing.com

STERLING and the distinctive Sterling logo are registered trademarks of
Sterling Publishing Co., Inc.

First published in France as *Les tribulations d'une caissière* by Éditions Stock
Copyright © Éditions Stock, 2008
English translation by Morag Young
English translation copyright © Gallic Books 2009
First published in Great Britain in 2009 by Gallic Books,
134 Lots Road, London, SW10 0RJ

Library of Congress Cataloging-in-Publication Data Available

2 4 6 8 10 9 7 5 3 1

Published by Sterling Publishing Co., Inc.
387 Park Avenue South, New York, NY 10016
Distributed in Canada by Sterling Publishing
c/o Canadian Manda Group, 165 Dufferin Street,
Toronto, Ontario, Canada M6K 3H6

Sterling ISBN 978-1-4027-7659-5

For information about custom editions, special sales, premium and
corporate purchases, please contact Sterling Special Sales
Department at 800-805-5489 or specialsales@sterlingpublishing.com.

Contents

For my brother, Gwenael. I wish I could have shared this book with you.

And for all those men and women who have worked behind the register.

Introduction

My name is Anna. I'm thirty-one years old with a degree in literature and a life story that is both completely ordinary and a little unusual. I've worked for eight years in a supermarket. I started out there just to fund my studies and to have some financial independence, but when I couldn't find any work using my degree, I stayed on and became that stalwart of modern life: a cashier.

The register. Not a great conversationalist, unless you count the beeps it makes when you scan the produce. As a result of listening to that robotic noise, I felt frankly that I was becoming a little like a robot myself. The fleeting interaction with the customers was not enough to make me feel human. Happily, though, contact with my colleagues did just that.

One day I decided to write about my working life and record the little incidents that fill the day of a cashier. Suddenly, I was looking differently at the customers filing past my register. I was seeing the world of retail with new eyes and discovering that it was a lot more varied than I had thought. There are the easy customers and the more challenging ones. Rich ones, poor ones. Nervous customers, boastful customers. Customers who treat you as if you were invisible and customers who say "hello." Some are always champing at the bit for the store to open, and some always arrive just as the store is closing. There are customers who flirt with you and customers who insult you. Who says nothing ever happens in the life of a cashier?

In this volume, I have put together a few of the most hilarious, hair-raising, baffling, and gratifying stories from my life behind the register. So it's time to take your shopping cart and enter the exciting life of a supermarket cashier. Look, the doors are already opening!

Happy shopping!

Welcome to the Wonderful World of Retail— and Your Dream Job

Congratulations! You've finally managed to get an interview and have actually been hired. Welcome to the retail family. You are now a cashier—sorry, checkout *operator*. That feels much more important, doesn't it?

The interview lasted only a couple of minutes, long enough for you to repeat what's already on your résumé and fill out some tax forms. IQ tests? A bit of mental arithmetic? Surely not. You'll be suggesting that they analyze your handwriting next. Need I remind you? You're going to work at the checkout—you're not being called to the Bar.

It's only your first day, but you still have to prove your worth. So let's get cracking. Time for training! Don't worry: an "old hand" will take you under her wing for at least, I don't know, a quarter of an hour? A morning if you're lucky. Two days if your manager is nice. There are some nice managers; I promise. It's just the luck of the draw.

Let's start with a tour of the store. It won't take long (besides, there are other things to be getting on with). There's the locker room, the break room, the waste disposal area with the Dumpsters, where all the produce that's past its sell-by date ends up—you'll find you spend a lot of time here—the office where you'll be given your cash drawer, and . . . well, that's it.

Now you know enough about the store to get down to work. You'll have plenty of time to explore your new workplace further during your breaks. It will make them more fun.

The first time you approach the register in your wonderful Chanel or Dior uniform or your hideous apron (depending on the store and the kind of customers that management wants to attract) with your cash drawer under your arm (the equivalent of several days' salary, no less), you are bound to feel a bit intimidated. Take a deep breath. That feeling will pass.

So you've found your register, organized your cash drawer, and settled in. You're really concentrating and really motivated. The "old hand" is beside you and you're all ears. You're ready to work. Not a moment too soon.

The main things to remember are: scan each item (with a quick glance to check that the price looks correct), add up the total, tell the customer, ask for a club card, take payment, ask for ID if necessary, give the customer his change, and give him the receipt—all with a nice, sincere smile. Then, "Thank-you-have-a-nice-day," and on to the next customer. Shall I go through it again?

In the beginning, it might seem that you have to work fast—too fast—especially if you start on a busy day. But it'll soon become automatic, and you won't pay too much attention to what you're doing. Within a month, it will seem as if you and your register are one.

✳✳✳

Time has flown by and the "old hand" is giving you less and less advice. It's all sinking in. You're becoming an expert at scanning items and giving change. Well done! It's really not that complicated; you just need to know what to do and when, and the rest comes of its own accord.

Now the "old hand" is leaving you to manage on your own. You'll be able to scan your first items independently. Hooray! What a treat that will be.

Actually, apart from the bee-eep of the scanner, it's not very exciting. Fortunately, there's lots of interaction with customers (be patient—more on that later).

Oh, yes, I almost forgot. There's a part that's not that easy but, strangely, it's quite interesting. You have to learn all the code numbers by heart for items that are sold by the unit: lemons, peppers, garlic, artichokes, etc. Don't panic. There aren't that many, and if you forget, there is a prompt sheet at the register. And you can always ask your colleagues—Jessica, Emma, Kate, Mark, Sarah, Justin—who are never far away. Try not to forget their names (not easy when you have about a hundred colleagues).

✳✳✳

4 * CHECKOUT GIRL

Your first day is almost over. The stragglers are leaving and the store is closing. So what are your first impressions? Actually, it's quite a fun job. You scan lots of items (and discover things you didn't know how to use or that even existed), you chat with pleasant colleagues, you listen to music all day, and it's nice and warm.

A dream job. Well, almost. You have to come back and do it all again tomorrow. And the day after. And the day after that. And, as time goes by, getting up in the morning to go to your dream job won't be quite so appealing.

Believe me.

2

The Top Three Questions Asked at the Register

Pay attention, please. This store's exclusive welcome gift to you is a set of the top three customer questions:

- ☛ "Where is the bathroom?"
- ☛ "How much cash can I get back?"
- ☛ "Are you open?"

Out of context, they're not so bad. But wait until you're behind your register. By the end of the day, these questions will make you want to commit an act of violence (or, at the very least, have a good scream). Judge for yourself.

The Most Urgent Question: "Where is the bathroom?"

CUSTOMER (*rushing up and usually quite flustered*)
Where is the bathroom?

CASHIER *(obliged to interrupt her conversation with another customer)*
Hello!

The customer does not reply.

CASHIER *(sighing inwardly)*
Over there.

And she points at the big glossy "Restrooms" sign hanging just opposite the registers. The customer rushes off. No "thank you" or "good-bye" or even "damn it." Takes too long. When you've got to go . . .

The Most Controversial Question: "How much cash can I get back?"

Ah, the debit card. It is convenient, fits neatly in one's pocket, and has made those messy green bills completely obsolete. Unfortunately, the ability to pay by debit card has been followed by the implicit notion that a supermarket is now a bank. As a cashier, you will encounter customers who come into your lane with a pack of gum and expect to be able to receive hundreds of dollars back when they pay by debit, presumably to fund the rest of their evening's activities—or perhaps to purchase a small island. If you were starting to get bored with your cashier position, congratulations! You've just moved on to the highly coveted job of bank teller. On a Saturday night, you might be lucky enough to experience the following:

CASHIER *(who has scanned the customer's copy of* US Weekly*)*
$3.99, please.

The customer whips out his debit card.

CUSTOMER *(who is talking loudly on his cell phone about the bar full of "hotties" he's about to "hit")*
How much cash can I get back?

CASHIER *(preparing to enter the world of finance)*
Twenty dollars.

CUSTOMER *(glaring up from his phone)*
I need two hundred.

CASHIER *(channeling her inner Gordon Gekko)*
I'm sorry, but the limit is twenty.

CUSTOMER
What the hell am I supposed to do with twenty dollars?

CASHIER *(pointing to the sign below the card scanner that says "$20 cash-back limit")*
I'm sorry, sir, but I can't give you more than twenty dollars.

CUSTOMER *(digging through his pocket and finding only three sticks of gum and a waitress's phone number)* Whatever. Keep your crappy magazine. I'm never shopping here again!

The customer furiously slams down his magazine and storms off. The cashier silently laments this most unfortunate loss of business before moving on to the next customer . . . who eagerly awaits with a pack of breath mints and a debit card.

The Most Annoying Question: "Are you open?"

So you aim to be the best, most polite, and friendliest cashier? OK, that's your right and it's very admirable (although don't forget how little you're paid). But promise me that you will never let anyone address you as if you were your register. You are a human being, not a machine that beeps.

Not only customers have rights. Here are a few suggestions as to how to deal with confused customers:

CUSTOMER
Are you open?

THE POLITE CASHIER
I'm not, but my register is.

THE SARCASTIC CASHIER
Beeeeeep!

THE FLIRTY CASHIER (*if the customer is really good-looking*)
Try me and see.

THE CASHIER WITH HER BEST SMILE
Are *you*?

I can't guarantee what reaction you'll get to any of the above. However, you will find that some customers vary the question:

- ☛ "Are you closed?"
- ☛ "Is she open?"
- ☛ "Are you available?"
- ☛ "Can I come over to you?"

It's up to you how to respond.

3

A Haute Couture Fashion Show

Do you care about your appearance? Do you hate uniforms? I'm sorry to have to remind you then that even though cashiers stand behind registers, that is not enough to identify them as cashiers. To avoid any confusion, you have to wear a uniform. Anyway, how else would you feel like you are part of a big family, the big brand family of the chain you work for? Your uniform is essential if you are to give your best.

Here are the various spring/summer/autumn/winter collections that await you.

The "Glamorous" Uniform

Did you dream of being a flight attendant when you were little? If so, this outfit will make you feel that your dream has been fulfilled. A budget airline, though—I hope that's OK. You could also use this navy blazer and skirt for a wedding, bar mitzvah, or award ceremony. Isn't life great?

Don't make any abrupt movements, however. The stitches

(made in China) are fragile and, frankly, the clothes aren't very well cut.

The Unisex Uniform

Do you need something to wear to take out the garbage? Now you have just the thing, thanks to these wonderful shapeless smocks, size XXL. They come in a wide assortment of colors. Depending on which hue your particular establishment chooses, you may be mistaken for a hospital orderly, a garbage collector, or a resident of a senior citizens' home. If you're a woman with short hair, you may want to consider some dangly earrings, lest you be mistaken for a man. (If you're a man with long hair . . . well, a flaming skull tattoo is always an option, with the added bonus of scaring away certain uppity clientele.) This generic uniform is certain to rid you of those pesky feelings of individualism and style. Remember (trust me, it won't be easy to forget) that you're a cashier, not a supermodel.

The Theme Uniform

Is your supermarket quirky and unique—and looking for any opportunity to show off? If so, be prepared to be the store's fashion plate. Perhaps your store is eager to convince customers that they are shopping at a local farm instead of at a generic chain. Your uniform: extra-large overalls in colors ranging from electric blue to piglet pink. (Women, whether you're pregnant or not, people will assume you're eight months along—or, if you're a man, that you're obese.) Or perhaps management is looking to create a shopping experience so jovial and uplifting that customers will think they've taken hallucinogenic drugs. Your attire: a bright red jacket over a shirt of vile green, patterned with large flowers, and wide pants of an indefinable color. All that's missing is the red nose. The customers certainly won't miss you. But you'll hope your friends will, so don't encourage them to stop by— you'll never hear the end of it.

The Cheap Uniform

Here we have a polo shirt with a sleeveless vest or apron, made in Taiwan, and vaguely in the chain's colors (before washing, that is). This garb is worn by all employees of the store, regardless of their role. The stores that favor this style are experts at saving the pennies. Better hope it's one of these stores that offers you a job. Besides, of all the options, you will look slightly less ridiculous in this outfit than in the others. I won't go any further than that. And the feeling of belonging to a big family will be even more pronounced.

In any event, avoid looking at yourself too often in the mirror at work if you don't want to have a breakdown or be forced to resist the urge to laugh like a madman in front of every customer.

4

Cashing Out: The Search
for the Missing Coin

It is 9:05 p.m. That was your first real day. You have just served your last and 289th customer. You've been behind the register for eight hours with two ten-minute breaks and a half-hour for lunch. You're tired. You dream of one thing: going to bed and sleeping until 6 a.m. tomorrow.

Wake up! The day isn't over yet!

You still have to clean your workstation (you weren't naive enough to think that a maintenance worker was going to do it for you, were you?) and cash out (you didn't have the gall to think that you were being paid to do nothing, did you?). Count yourself lucky: at least you don't have to clean the aisles!

Hurry over to the office with your cash drawer. Sit down with your colleagues and find a pen and paper. Don't yawn—you haven't finished work yet! Start by counting your coins, then your bills, and finally your coin rolls. (I say "your" but, obviously, they're not *really* yours.) Actually, count them in whatever order you please—you still have the power to make that choice. Don't let yourself be distracted by the chatter, the

15

doors opening and closing, and the rattling of coins. Concentrate, or you'll regret it when you find yourself with the joy of recounting.

Not enough light? Don't complain. The soft "mood" lighting is much preferable to the blinding, fluorescent glare of the store.

Fifteen minutes later: OK, you have scrupulously noted how many pennies, nickels, dimes, and quarters you have. And the number of one-dollar, five-dollar, ten-dollar, twenty-dollar, fifty-dollar, and hundred-dollar bills. And the number of coin rolls . . . Calm down, now. Yes, you have a small fortune in your hands. But don't think about that. Instead, think about your paycheck at the end of the week. That will bring you back down to earth again.

Add it all up and then subtract the one hundred dollars in cash that was in your cash drawer at the start of the day.

SUPERVISOR
173, how much? 173?! Yes, that's you!

CASHIER
I have a name!

SUPERVISOR
Yes, I know, but it's quicker this way. So, 173?

CASHIER
$3,678.65!

SUPERVISOR
Count again, 173; you've made a mistake! I warned you. You weren't concentrating properly.

CASHIER
Am I way off? Or just a little? Under? Over?

SUPERVISOR
Just count it again.

Ten minutes later:

CASHIER
$3,678.15!

SUPERVISOR
OK. Before you go, make sure that your checks and coupons are safely put away. And not in your underwear.

9:35 p.m. You take off your uniform in the locker room. You have only five minutes to catch your bus. Good night and sweet dreams (full of beeeeps, hellos, good-byes . . .).

✶ ✶ ✶

Now, if you're lucky, you may work in a store that simplifies this process for you. (After all, you're just a cashier; you shouldn't be burdened—or trusted—with tasks like counting large quantities of money.) Someone from the office may come and remove large bills from your drawer throughout your shift, so that, should an armed robber enter your lane, it will just be your well-being that's at risk and not too much of the store's money. Quite thoughtful of management, really. Or a front-end manager may use a special machine to weigh the bills and coins in your drawer to determine how much money it contains. The good news is that at the end of your shift, you can just lock up your drawer and go home. The bad news: if the computer determines you are short at the end of the day, you have little recourse. And the worst part of such highly computerized systems? If there is a power outage, hopefully you like your store, because you're not going anywhere for a while. Of course, for the truly dedicated cashier, there's nowhere you'd rather be.

5

The Job Interview

I've forgotten to mention something very important about your job interview. It doesn't matter if you have never worked before, you don't know how to count, or you are agoraphobic or afraid of the dark as long as you are available immediately, you accept the wonderful salary offered, you have a social security number, and you can answer this question: "Why do you want to work with us?"

Yes, even to be a cashier, you have to come up with a good reason. Try one of the following:

"Because I've always dreamed of working in a supermarket!"

If you want them to believe you, say it with a lot of conviction and make your eyes sparkle with enthusiasm at the same time. Not easy.

"Because my mother was a cashier!"

Same conviction and enthusiasm required as for the previous suggestion.

"Because, like you, I want to 'make life taste better'" or "Because, as you say, 'Every little bit helps!'"

Stretching it a little, I know, but such devotion is always well received. So you might as well. You have to be careful, though. Not all the slogans work. Be wary of passing yourself off as "everyone's favorite ingredient."

"I'm a student. I need a part-time job to support myself."

The classic answer but very convincing. And managers really like students. They grumble less than old people do and don't mind working on weekends. So it's an excellent answer. Of course, if you're not actually a student, you have to look young enough to be credible. You shouldn't have too much of a problem up to the age of thirty or thirty-five.

"I need a job to survive."

Avoid this answer—even if it's true, the manager will think you're "not very motivated," "lacking team spirit," and "unsuited to the store's commercial ambitions," and your application risks being relegated to the bottom of the pile (which is enormous, by the way).

But there are many answers that will impress. For inspiration, pretend that you're applying to be a lawyer instead of a cashier. Come on; use your imagination!

6

Yours Statistically ✂

Here are a few things to ponder if you are to be an unbeatable cashier:

- About 2.5 million people work for supermarkets in the United States. (You'll be joining a nice big family!)
- 15–20 items must be scanned every minute. This can increase to 45 at some discount chains.

So the cashier has to handle customers shopping without proper consideration, leading to damaged goods if customers can't keep up with the pace, which, of course, is nearly always the case. Well, they're not paid according to their performance—but neither is the cashier, actually.

- 500 to 1,000 items are scanned per hour.
- Approximately 15,000 to 30,000 items are scanned per week.
- Six thousand pounds of goods are lifted per hour (more on good days).
- Almost ninety tons of goods are lifted per week.
- Per year? Get out your calculator (not provided by your store).

Do I look like a bodybuilder? Well, hardly. Quite often I feel about seventy.

Every week you can consult the Items per Minute board in the break room so that you can see which cashiers have collected the most money and whether you have been a tortoise or a hare. Don't panic. There's no reward (not even a bottle of ketchup) for the winner. But your parents and children will be really proud of you.

✳✳✳

Every day you will say (on average):
- ☞ 250 hellos
- ☞ 250 good-byes
- ☞ 500 thank-yous
- ☞ 200 Do you have a club cards
- ☞ 70 Please swipe your cards
- ☞ 70 Please enter your PINs
- ☞ 30 The restrooms are over theres

. . . and many other similarly poetic lines. You're not a robot, are you? Of course not! A robot doesn't smile.
- ☞ Your average monthly pay: $8.59 per hour
- ☞ Average hours per week: 29.4

But let's get one thing straight. Don't think you'll be able to supplement your hours with part-time work. Your manager will ensure that your schedule will change every week. Of course, you could always work as a housekeeper from 5 a.m. until 8 a.m. or take in ironing. You didn't want any time for family, did you? Well done; you've chosen the ideal job.

Here's an example of an average week:

☛ Monday: 9 a.m. to 2:30 p.m. (working time: 5 hours 30 minutes; break time: 10 minutes)

☛ Tuesday: off

☛ Wednesday: 3 p.m. to 8:45 p.m. (working time: 5 hours 45 minutes; break time: 10 minutes)

☛ Thursday: 11:30 a.m. to 3:30 p.m. (working time: 4 hours; break time: 10 minutes)

☛ Friday: 3:15 p.m. to 9 p.m. (working time: 5 hours 45 minutes; break time: 10 minutes)

☛ Saturday: 9 a.m. to 1 p.m. and 4:30 p.m. to 9:15 p.m. (working time: 8 hours 45 minutes; break time: 10 minutes and 10 minutes)

The following week? Don't worry; your hours will be completely different. If you work at a highly organized store, you might receive your new schedule on a certain day each week. Otherwise, you'll be told your new schedule anywhere from three weeks in advance, if the person who creates the schedule is particularly zealous, to twenty-four hours in advance if a lot of cashiers are away.

Laws governing meals and rest breaks vary from state to state. In many states, four hours is the maximum number of hours you can work on the register without a break (in theory, although some employment contracts contravene this).

Depending where you work, four hours behind the register may earn you a ten-minute break. (If you're lucky, your union may negotiate a whopping fifteen-minute break instead.) Feeling hungry during a four-hour shift? Well, you can forget about a nice hot meal—not if you want to eat *and* go to the bathroom. Perish the thought!

So there you have it. That's your dream job—is it all you hoped it would be? You have the supermarkets to thank for that.

7

"Hang on a Minute; I'm at the Register!"

Ah, mobile phones. What marvelous inventions. It's just incredible all the things they can do: play music, show TV, send e-mail, follow the stock market . . . Incidentally, they also enable us to make calls when and where we want. But that's not all mobile phones can do. Some can even make a man (or a woman) invisible—and it's not only the most expensive models that can do it. The fact that cashiers are pretty invisible anyway helps with this trick.

CUSTOMER (*on the phone, talking loudly as if he were on his own at home*)
But I'm already at the checkout! Couldn't you have told me earlier that you wanted bananas?

CASHIER (*very loudly to remind him that he is at the checkout and not at home*)
Hello!

CUSTOMER *(apparently he still thinks he's at home)*
Go out tonight? Are you feeling better, then?

CASHIER *(who has worked quickly so that the customer soon will be at home)*
$13.59, please.

CUSTOMER *(collecting his shopping with one hand and not moving quickly at all)*
I'm sure it's a stomach bug. I hope you haven't given it to me. I don't want to spend all night on the toilet.

CASHIER *(clearing her throat and speaking very loudly)*
$13.59, please!

CUSTOMER *(with a quick glance at the cashier but continuing calmly to collect his groceries)*
You're the one who never listens to me. You should wash your hands every time you go out.

CASHIER *(clenching her fists and speaking really, really loudly)*
Do you have a club card?

CUSTOMER *(inserting his debit card into the machine without glancing up)*
I get it. I'm not deaf. You're so grumpy when you're sick.

The customer grabs the receipt from the cashier's hand as if she were a ticket machine.

CUSTOMER (*moving away with his shopping, still on the phone, and still talking loudly*)
It's a good thing everyone's not like you.

CASHIER (*really loud, but only in her head*)
And it's a good thing everyone's not like you. What an idiot!

She decides not to bother with a good-bye. Every small victory counts.

Don't feel sorry for yourself. You've just had an unforgettable experience — for a few minutes you have been completely invisible. Look on the bright side: you might get to experience the same thing again but with a subtle difference.

CUSTOMER (*on the phone*)
Blah, blah, blah . . .

CASHIER
Hello!

CUSTOMER (*looking at the cashier*)
Hello. (*His eyes immediately focus elsewhere.*) So, as I was saying . . . blah, blah, blah . . .

I'm not exaggerating. But there really is a reason to look on the bright side. It's not impossible that you will come across this rare specimen:

CUSTOMER *(on the phone)*
I'll call you back; I'm at the register.

The customer hangs up and puts his phone away.

CASHIER *(with a really big, sincere smile)*
Hello!

CUSTOMER *(returning the smile)*
Hello!

Isn't life great? Well, yes, but don't get carried away. That kind of customer is very, very, very rare. Cashiers who have met them still talk about it.

Now, if you are particularly sensitive about appearing invisible and this is your second year behind the register (surely you're used to it by now?!), you might want to do this instead:

CUSTOMER *(on the phone)*
Blah, blah, blah . . .

CASHIER *(scanning products quickly while . . . talking on her hands-free device)*
Blah, blah, blah . . .

CUSTOMER *(looking at the cashier)*
Where's the bathroom?

CASHIER *(points in a general direction without glancing at the customer)*
As I was saying, blah, blah, blah . . .

In your dreams—no, not even in your dreams. A cashier must always act like a cashier, and a cashier does not use the phone at work! At least not until computers have replaced her entirely. Some customers appear to think they already have.

🔒

r---

Entertaining the
Supermarket

L---

If the melodic bee-eeps of the register, the clanking of carts, or
the dull hum of cell phone chatter fails to entertain you, you
can look forward to the riveting announcements that blast (or
sometimes crackle) from the PA system. Not every supermarket still employs the supermarket announcer—part master of
ceremonies, part game-show host. If yours does, prepare for
some lively entertainment.

This strange specimen is wheeled out on very special
occasions: Mother's Day, Father's Day, the first day of spring,
Independence Day, Thanksgiving, St. Patrick's Day, Valentine's Day, Groundhog Day, Cinco de Mayo, etc. You'll soon
learn that any occasion is a good excuse for a party. And on
those days how you will regret not being a customer . . .

You'll soon discover that not just anyone can stop customers in their tracks and lure them to the daily specials.
Whether it's Joe from the fish counter enthusiastically declar-
ing it Fish Friday or a behind-the-curtain Wizard of Oz
character rhapsodizing about the day's two-for-one specials,
supermarket announcers need nice voices (well, voices) and a

lot of endurance. They have to be able to talk into their micro-
phones all day long (which will rapidly make you detest them).

They also have to be convincing.

ANNOUNCER (*into the microphone*)
Ladies and gentlemen, today we have a wonderful, magnificent, sublime, gigantic, special offer:
buy two sausages and get the third free! Wonderful
value if you're planning a superb, magnificent family
barbecue!

They must be good at the schmaltz.

ANNOUNCER
Ah, a family barbecue. What could be nicer than a
family barbecue? What could be more touching? So
don't forget, tomorrow is Mother's Day. Do something
nice for Mom! For only $2.99!

They must enjoy travel.

ANNOUNCER
Don't miss today's special tasting in the bread-
products aisle. Today only, you can sample French

pastries, lovingly made by artisans: croissants, *pains au chocolat*, *pains aux raisins*, and more!

They have to have the charm of Regis Philbin (generally, they think they *are* Regis Philbin).

ANNOUNCER (*to a customer*)
So, madam, what is the capital of France? Paris, Berlin, or Madrid? The right answer will win you this wonderful, amazing, magnificent meat thermometer.

CUSTOMER
Um, I don't know.

ANNOUNCER
Do you want to phone a friend?

(*The announcer laughs heartily as he says this—announcers also need a sense of humor.*)

CUSTOMER
OK.

ANNOUNCER
OK, I'm your friend. Here's a clue: it starts with *P*.

CUSTOMER
Philadelphia!

ANNOUNCER (*surprised*)
Uh . . . no. The answer was Paris. But never mind,
madam. Since it's Mother's Day tomorrow, you win
this wonderful, amazing, magnificent bouquet of
flowers!

Finally, they need to be resourceful.

ANNOUNCER (*into the microphone*)
Little Johnny has lost his mom and dad. Could they
come quickly to the pet-food aisle? Their little boy
really needs to go to the bathroom!

So, you see, it's true. Not everyone has the skills to be
a supermarket announcer. You will come to admire them for
their ability to make so much of so little. It's a high-wire act!

9

I've Saved a Place

Some people have a real phobia about waiting in line. But how can you avoid it at the supermarket, or the post office for that matter? With subtle little ploys, that's how. Here are the most devious:

Tactic 1

DEVIOUS CUSTOMER (*running up with four items in his hand*)
Are you open?

CASHIER
I'm not, but my register is! Hello!

DEVIOUS CUSTOMER
Excellent!

The customer's four items are scanned.

CASHIER
$8.27, please.

DEVIOUS CUSTOMER
Hang on; my girlfriend's just coming—she forgot something.

Five minutes later, still no girlfriend in sight and the line of customers is building up behind him.

CASHIER *(sensing the mounting tension)*
Can I ask you to wait to one side?

DEVIOUS CUSTOMER *(who's oblivious to the tension but annoyed by the question)*
She's coming! Can't you wait just a second?

Indeed, at that moment the cashier sees her arrive with . . . two baskets filled to the brim.

CUSTOMER BEHIND THE DEVIOUS CUSTOMER
Don't mind me!

The cashier privately thinks the waiting customer is right to be aggrieved.

DEVIOUS CUSTOMER
I've been waiting, too, you know, like everyone else!

Tactic 2

The devious customer runs up with her cart and starts to empty it on to the conveyor belt.

> **CASHIER**
> Hello!

But the devious customer has already disappeared, leaving her cart still half full. The cashier tells herself that she'll be back in a minute and starts scanning the items on the conveyor belt. Another customer arrives.

> **CASHIER** (*conciliatory*)
> Hello! The person in front of you will be back in just a minute.

The other customer sighs. Two minutes later there is still no sign of the first customer.

> **CUSTOMER 2** (*not happy*)
> I've got other things to do, you know!

> **CASHIER** (*embarrassed*)
> She'll be right back. I promise.

Two minutes later, still no one.

CUSTOMER 2 (*aggressive*)
This is beyond a joke!

CASHIER (*very, very embarrassed*)
I'm sorry.

CUSTOMER 2
Sorry! Well, that's not good enough. I'm changing lanes. This is outrageous!

The second customer changes lanes just as the devious customer calmly returns with her arms full.

DEVIOUS CUSTOMER
If I'd known you had no one waiting, I wouldn't have rushed!

Tactic 3

The cashier has no one at her register and indicates to an elderly customer waiting nearby that she should come to her lane. The customer hurries over as quickly as she is able, but when she is almost there, a man rushes up and does a flashy fishtail move with his cart. He immediately starts putting his shopping on the conveyor belt.

CASHIER
Excuse me, sir, but this lady was here before you.

DEVIOUS CUSTOMER *(without so much as a glance at the lady in question)*
You're joking! Hurry up; I don't have all day.

The elderly customer indicates to the cashier that it doesn't matter. Shame.

Tactic 4

The cashier serves several customers and then turns to find an empty cart without an owner. Five other customers are waiting behind.

CASHIER *(to the customer behind the empty cart)*
Come forward, please.

As the cashier is serving the first customer in line, the owner of the empty cart rushes up with two baskets full of groceries and quickly pushes her way to the front.

FIRST CUSTOMER
Excuse me, but I was here before you!

VERY DEVIOUS CUSTOMER *(pointing at the empty cart)*
Excuse me, but I was here before you!

If the first customer decides not to let this go, the atmosphere will turn ugly very quickly. Abuse will fly and a fight could break out. Frankly, the very devious customer has behaved so badly that you'd have to be a saint to stay calm. The cashier, with the best seat in the house, keeps score as they duke it out.

I would advise all these very devious customers to do their shopping on the Internet. They will find it less tiring.

10

Kissing Couples

So, you thought supermarkets weren't the sexiest of places? Think again.

They are much more erotic places than you had imagined. You'll be surprised by how many kisses are stolen in the aisles (including the toilet-paper aisle), by the number of languorous glances exchanged at the butcher's counter, by the number of hands on bottoms in the frozen-food section, by the number of breasts (and more, if the chemistry is right) fondled in the produce aisle, and by the romantic and even passionate conversations in front of the cheese counter. You'll be surprised, as well, by the number of domestic disputes.

Why? Maybe the plethora of products all within arm's reach excites the senses.

Once it was my good fortune to witness real passion. It was the end of the day. Most people had gone. There was no one at my register (yes, it does happen). I was looking around and my glance fell on a couple and their four children in the magazine aisle. I was immediately struck by the great tenderness between Mom and Dad, and I thought to myself that to be so in love after four children was the stuff of dreams.

I started daydreaming at my register. Lots of romantic images passed through my mind until a sound like the unblocking of a sink made me look up. My dream couple was walking toward me with their cart and four children . . . and wildly making out. Hence the romantic noise.

I told myself that love is deaf as well as blind. It can't afford to wait, either. All the time they were at my register, they were fondling each other. And completely without inhibition—they weren't worried about anyone catching sight of Mom's pink lacy G-string or Dad's very hairy buttocks. Their children, unmoved, left them to it and took care of packing the shopping. I suppose it's better than parents who argue. But, I have to admit, I blushed. It's not every day that such passion takes place in front of your register.

✳✳✳

In your role as hostess of this love shack, you should expect to arouse desire, too (even though your uniform is horrible). Be prepared for these grand declarations of love:

CASHIER
$99.40, please. Do you have a club card?

CUSTOMER (*enterprisingly*)
Do you want to sleep with me tonight?

Others will be slightly less direct, a little shyer, and a bit more obsessive, too. They will come to your register nineteen times in one week, each time with just one item. Eyes always on the floor. No hello or good-bye. You'll start wondering if they're a bit crazy. But on the twentieth occasion:

CUSTOMER (*white as a sheet*)
Could . . . could I . . . I . . . buy you a drink?

If you say no, you'll break his heart but save your own. The rejected admirer will generally run away without asking for his change. And you will stand there with your mouth open, taken aback by the turn of events.

Exciting, isn't it?

11

"Embarrassing" Items

What embarrasses or intimidates customers? Nothing, you say—isn't that the nature of customers? Well, let me put you straight because there are a few items that bother some customers. Thanks to these items, you get a little insight into those dear customers' personalities. You will laugh, but only inside.

Toilet Paper

Everyone uses it (the United States alone spends more than six billion dollars a year on toilet paper). Yet, for some customers it's as if their toilet paper smells bad already. You barely have time to scan it (don't be sadistic and pretend you can't find the bar code) before they grab it from you and bury it at the bottom of their cart or bag under their other shopping. They will breathe easy again only once they are sure "it" can't be seen. And if "it" can still be seen (because the bag is too small or the thirty-two-roll family pack is too large), they will try their best for several seconds to push "it" out of sight. Others will desperately try to find newspapers to cover it. And they will all scuttle away from your register as quickly as possible.

Sanitary Napkins

Apparently, for some girls (and even those who aren't girls anymore), periods are still a shameful illness. Luckily, sanitary-napkin packaging and tampon boxes are more discreet than toilet paper and can quickly be stowed in bags—but not before you've seen these customers blush furiously, mumble an embarrassed "hello" with their eyes on their shoes, and drop their change in their nervousness. It's as if you had suddenly become a very imposing person. Amazing—a cashier can actually intimidate his customers! Then there are those for whom it is such an insurmountable ordeal that they prefer to send their husband or boyfriend to buy them. Generally, these men find it rather amusing.

But you shouldn't be surprised by any of this. When you think of all the commercials that systematically highlight bad smells and leaks that will make everyone look at you, it's no wonder that some people feel ashamed.

Condoms
(My Favorite "Embarrassing" Item)

There are, of course, the customers who appear to think, "If I hide this box of condoms, no one will see it." They try to "drown" the box among other items (some will even make sure that they choose other products whose color and packaging are similar to the condom box's), or they throw it down on the conveyor belt at the last minute like a casual afterthought. But they should beware of throwing it too hard, because it might end up on the conveyor belt of the register next door where their neighbor is paying for her shopping. If that happens, their only recourse is to move to South America.

Then there are customers who don't give a damn. But they aren't funny.

In addition, there are the show-offs. Real comedians. Pumped full of testosterone, they put two or even three or four boxes of XXL condoms on the conveyor belt. They don't buy anything else, obviously, unless it's lubricating jelly, and they fully expect all the customers around them (and preferably the whole store) to notice and look at them with admiration (if they're ladies) and jealousy (if they're men). They won't like you if you scan their boxes too quickly, but they will love you if you use your microphone to ask the price (specifying that it's XXL). And, obviously, they never use a bag.

Fattening Foods

This embarrassing purchase mostly applies to "big-boned" women who secretly like to indulge in cookies, potato chips, ice cream . . . and that's just Monday night's snack. Yet they don't want to expose their cart full of decadent delights to their friends, neighbors, or the good-looking single dad parked behind them in line. Hence the tub of chocolate ice cream casually buried beneath the asparagus, the chocolate-fudge cookies camouflaged in rice cakes, and the boxes of clearance Valentine's Day chocolates, still lingering in the store close to St. Patrick's Day, subtly hidden among the customer's fat-free yogurts and cottage cheese. Try not to snicker when you witness two "friends" who have run into each other on line covertly peering into each other's carts and furtively trying to push their cartons of strawberries and fat-free milk to the top. Resist the temptation to grab their guiltiest pleasures out of their carts and announce over the loudspeaker, "Price check on chocolate-dipped potato chips, doughnut-flavored ice cream . . . and super-size tampons." Your customer may not show you her appreciation, but the universe will reward you for your restraint.

Ah, so many unforgettable experiences await you!

12

I'm Hungry!

At lunchtime you often see customers using their lunch break to do their shopping, but you also see others (and it might be the same ones) just popping in for a bite. The supermarket starts to look like a self-service café . . . and some customers, a little like pigs.

Maybe it could be a new retail concept.

Imagine having this gang of gluttons at your register:

Customer 1

He's in the process of devouring his tuna salad sandwich—noisily with his mouth wide open so that you can see everything inside (hey, where are the cucumbers?). You ask him if you can borrow his sandwich for a second to scan the price. You have to wait for him to bite another piece off before he hands it to you, and he takes it back almost immediately. Mind your fingers. He pays and thanks you with some incomprehensible words accompanied by pieces of tuna and bread, which land on your conveyor belt. Wonderful; you get to use your paper towel and cleaning products sooner than you'd planned. But watch out: mayonnaise is slippery.

51

Customer 2

He puts his items on your belt, including a bag of chips, which you pick up. They spray all over your register because he hasn't thought it necessary to warn you that he has already opened the bag. On the other hand, he does find it necessary to shout at you (just what you need) and demand another bag of chips. While he goes to get it, give your register a quick clean. Don't worry if your hands are all greasy—they'll match your conveyor belt, which is already well coated.

Customer 3

You've noticed him in the line and already feel ill. You've seen him unwrap a family-size Camembert and bite straight into it. When it's his turn, he has already finished it. How can he have gobbled it all down at such speed? The smell is making you gag. And it will hang around long after the customer has gone.

Customer 4

This one shouts at you because you want to make her pay for the bottle of fruit juice she drank and left beside the register. It's true, of course, and you should never forget it: cashiers are supposed to be blind and stupid.

The lunch period requires nerves of steel and a strong stomach, but you'll soon get used to it. The sight of customers who eat in the aisles will no longer revolt you. One less thing to scan, you'll tell yourself.

Is it time for your lunch now? Bon appétit!

13

Bargain Hunters—Because Every Penny Counts!

I admire those customers (mostly female) who buy only the store's bargains and nothing else. Maybe it's their revenge for ever-rising prices and the feeling that they are being squeezed dry.

This kind of customer has an iron will. She has a long, detailed shopping list and never allows herself to be tempted by anything that is not on special offer. Standing in front of the cheese counter, she would like to buy Camembert, but only Roquefort is on sale. Neither she nor her husband like it much, but never mind; she takes it anyway. Four of them. Same thing for the fruit yogurts—only the strawberry flavor is covered by the manufacturer's coupon, and her son hates strawberry. She gets it anyway. "Strawberry flavor or no dessert."

She also plans ahead: the family-size laundry detergent— "Not satisfied? Money-back guarantee." Five containers. "It will always come in handy. There are three of us at home." The same thing for the flour—two for the price of one. Ten bags. "There'll be some left over for Christmas." (Even though it's only January.)

Finally, this type of customer has a lot of patience. On each trip, she meticulously checks all around the store to make sure she doesn't miss any bargains. But it's at the register that she really needs patience. She has come equipped with a foot-high pile of coupons (sometimes one for each item) and makes certain that all sale items are rung up properly—sometimes even demanding to see each specific discount on the receipt. So what if lots of people are waiting? That's not her problem. Luckily, the regulars come at quiet times and love sharing their discoveries with the cashiers.

Unfortunately, the obsessive frugality does not end once these customers leave the store. If you work at a large chain, chances are your store allows customers to return items for any reason, even without a receipt. And when these same customers come to return their defective purchases, they tend to arrive at the busiest times and with much less generosity toward the store's employees. Depending on your store, you may be able to point these aggrieved souls to the customer-service desk. Otherwise, you will have to contend with the customer who is dissatisfied because her cheese tastes "funny," or demands that you smell her meat to confirm it has a putrid odor, or complains that her cat won't touch the discount pet food she purchased as part of a two-for-one special. And just wait until you inform these customers that they must fill out a return receipt.

Well, what can you expect? You're not dealing with just any customer. The Bargain Hunter is well trained and well equipped, and she leaves no penny behind.

14

The Wonderful Club Card in All Its Complicated Simplicity

What's the point? There isn't one, or not much of one (don't kid yourself—it won't make you a millionaire). It's just an ingenious way to encourage customers to come back to a particular store instead of going to their competitors. Play your cards right, and you can earn a *free* turkey breast if you spend hundreds of dollars on groceries in the next two weeks! That is, if you keep track of your points on your mile-long receipt, printed in some elaborate shorthand only a pencil pusher in the corporate office and a few elite code breakers at the CIA can understand. What, you don't like turkey? Well, no worries. Next week your friendly supermarket is offering a free ham. Really makes you want to fight tooth and nail to get that supermarket club card, doesn't it? And makes it imperative that you go out and buy as many products as possible as often as possible.

But that's just scratching the surface of what the club card can give you. It also offers amazing discounts: ten dollars for ten boxes of elbow pasta, in case your daughter's entire kindergarten class decides to stop by for lunch one day; or, when you spend fifteen dollars on a certain brand of cereal, you'll mysteriously be mailed a five-dollar certificate toward your next grocery purchase, if you qualify and if you have a club card (I always admire the simplicity of their explanations, don't you?). Then there are the special-offer days when card-holders (aren't they lucky?) can buy more to spend more.

I admire the way the marketing people in supermarkets so readily (or should that be so disdainfully?) assume that their customers will react to club cards like children who have been presented with a new toy. (Look, here's a miniature version of your club card to hang on your key ring!) But, given the success of club cards, consumers do seem to have rediscovered their inner child. And today "the card" is essential. The more you have (any of them), the more you feel the supermarkets belong to you. But, above all, if we didn't have club cards, the cashiers wouldn't have anything to say to the customer. ("How does it work?" "Why doesn't it give me anything?" "How many points do I have?" "Will my club card work at my dentist's office?" "I didn't have my card with me last month—can you add my points?" and so on.) That really would be a shame.

15

Closing Time and Opening Time—What Fun!

"We would like to inform customers that the store will be closing in fifteen minutes. Please make your way to the registers. Have a nice evening."

8:45 p.m.

Panic buying. Customers go mad. There's not a minute to lose. People start running all over the place.

Bang! Carts collide with one another.

Crash! The chocolate-box pyramid falls down.

"Damn it, they've already packed up the green beans!"

Thud! Chuck the butter, milk, cheese, and yogurt in the cart . . . and never mind the rest.

"Why are they closing so early? Lazy bastards!"

8:55 p.m.

The music from the speakers stops.

"Quick; get to the register!"

Only three lanes still open. A few minutes to wait in line. "You'll have time to get some pasta while I wait!"

9 p.m.

The front doors start to close.

The last customer has exited. Oh, no! Here's another one running over, out of breath.

The lights start to go out.

That's it; the day really is over.

You let out a little sigh of relief, followed almost immediately by a cry of amazement. Who is that in the cracker aisle? There's a cart, right at the end. A couple is wandering up as if they have all the time in the world. You can tell from their attitude that they don't intend to head to the registers yet. But sparks are going to fly—the security guard has spotted them, too.

You can hear raised voices. The lady's face is all red. After a good five minutes, the argument stops and the couple follows the security guard, irritated. You think he's won. But suddenly, when they are only a few feet away from your register, the husband turns around and dashes back to get that box of crackers. A matter of life or death, apparently.

The woman continues to push her cart slowly, looking you straight in the eyes.

At the register, they are achingly slow and verbally abusive. One item scanned, one insult thrown at you. "It's a scandal. We're your best customers. We have the right to take our time to choose!" Another item scanned, another insult thrown at you. "Don't go so fast. Are you stupid or something?" Another item scanned, another insult . . . and their cart is full.

9:25 p.m.

The couple leaves your register. All the lights are out except yours, like a lighthouse fighting the wind and waves. You have been on overtime for twenty-five minutes. It's unpaid, but you can claim it back in leave when management feels like it. Smile—the couple comes back at least twice a month, and always at the same time. But, hey, the next time they come at closing time, you won't be there. It'll be your day off, you lucky thing!

A piece of advice: buy a punching bag!

***

There is also an opening-time version of this couple, and the countdown starts early:

8:25 a.m., Thirty-Five Minutes Before Opening

Their car arrives in the parking lot. They are the first customers. They beam with pride. They can park in the best spot, just in front of the entrance. The first victory of the day. Quick; there's no time to lose: get the best cart (sparkling clean inside and with no squeaky wheels).

Thirty Minutes Before Opening

They are in position—the front of their cart is touching the entrance barrier. It has started to rain. They have forgotten their umbrellas. But they won't wait in the car and risk having their place stolen when a second car arrives! The second victory of the day.

Fifteen Minutes Before Opening

They are soaked through but still the first of more than . . . six people. So that makes six victories so far. Their impatience and adrenaline mount. Their cart revs as they do a final check of the shopping list with simultaneous visualization of the store's aisles. Once inside, they mustn't lose a second. Careful! Raindrops are smudging the shopping list. Never mind; they know it by heart.

Five Minutes Before Opening

Your day begins. A big sigh followed by a long yawn. Your eyes are still puffy with sleep. You sit down with your cash drawer. You glance at the entrance and notice the seven . . . eight . . . ten . . . fifteen morning fanatics. You let out another big, long sigh.

One Minute Before Opening

The couple is dripping wet. "It's always the same at this place — they always open late!"

Opening Time

"Good morning and welcome to . . ." The noise of the security grating rising prevents the end of the welcome message from being heard. The couple: "Ah, at last!" The grating rises and rises . . . slowly, too slowly. They slip underneath. The security guard indicates that they should wait. "You're late. We've got other things to do, you know!" they say angrily.

Opening + Thirty Seconds

They (finally!) get through the door, the first to do so. There's not a second to lose. They head straight to the meat aisle. There won't be enough for everyone.

Opening + Four Minutes

They are your first customers. You record the first *beeeep!* of the day. Well done! You're impressed: thirty items collected in less than five minutes. That's a first. You watch them. They must be savoring their absolute victory. Well, no, actually. The husband is annoyed. "Can't you go a bit faster?"

Opening + Seven Minutes

They leave your register. With a "thank you" or "good-bye"? Anything? No time . . . the exit is at the other end of the store.

Opening + Eight Minutes

The exit security grating is not open yet. The couple is standing in front of it, furious. That makes your day.

Opening + Thirty Minutes

They have gone home and put their shopping away. Their hair is still wet. They have nothing else planned for the day. The husband sneezes. Outside, the rain has stopped. The sun comes out.

* * *

So which would you prefer: the Opening Time couple or the Closing Time couple? Can't decide? How about both in the same day?

16

What a Comedian

✄

Until now, I haven't given you a very positive image of customers. Let me rectify that by telling you about the ones who make you laugh. Hold on to your register . . . it's going to be really fun!

In the space of one day, on average you will hear:

☛ "Sorry to interrupt your rest!" eighteen times.

Eighteen times a day, you'll reply, "No rest for the wicked!"

☛ Seventeen times a day, you'll hear, "Were you waiting for me?"

Seventeen times a day, you'll reply, "Of course. I was starting to get worried!"

☛ Fifteen times, you'll hear, "If I'm nice, will you give me a good price?"

Fifteen times, you'll reply, "Do you want it twice or three times as expensive?"

☛ Ten times, you'll hear, "It's free, then!" (because the price won't scan).

Ten times, you'll reply, "Of course it is. Take the cart as well."

☛ Eight times, you'll hear, "I've bagged my groceries. Can I leave without paying?"

Eight times, you'll reply, "If you run fast!"

☛ Once, you'll be asked, "What do you call a camel with three humps?"

Once, you'll reply (even if you know the answer by heart), "I don't know. What do you call a camel with three humps?"

Once, the customer will answer, "Humphrey!"

☛ Once, someone will try to do an impersonation of a celebrity.

Once, you'll reply (in good faith), "The president?"

Once, the customer will reply, disappointed, "No, Regis Philbin!"

Don't look like that! At least they aren't nasty, and they actually acknowledge your presence. OK, being treated like an idiot isn't that fun. But if you don't answer, at least give them a little smile (I know, it'll encourage them to do it again next time).

By the way, do you know what the cashier's best feature is? It's her laugh!

17

A Healthy Mind in a Healthy Body

Ladies and gentlemen, are you fed up with your unsightly spare tires? Do you dream about losing your love handles? Are you finding it impossible to reach your ideal weight? Panic over: by working on the register, you have chosen the best possible path to weight loss. The miracle solution is at the end of the conveyor belt.

Let the Cashier Mind and Body™ laboratory guide you: follow these exercises, and your well-being will improve in record time.

Lose Weight

Your shifts will change every day and from one week to the next. The upside: you'll skip meals, leading to certain weight loss. Cashier Mind and Body™ has proved it.

Small downside: you must avoid snacking during your breaks. If the snack machine in the break room makes eyes at you, it'll quickly give you some extra padding that will keep you warm but will be fatal for your dream body! But your limitless willpower will keep you away from these servants of the devil and point you in the healthy direction of a bottle of mineral water (or tap water) and apples, your only indispensable workplace companions. Small downside: the noise of your stomach could rival the beep of your register.

Work Those Biceps

Ah, blessed be the stores that require you to lift heavy items onto the register to be scanned. Thanks to this additional effort, when you work on the register, you will be able to tone your arms beautifully. (Men, this exercise is especially beneficial right before beach season.) Your biceps will be endlessly grateful for these relentlessly repeated exercises. Be sure to keep up a good pace!

Small downside: Cashier Mind and Body™ has not been able to determine whether carrying heavy items can create tendonitis. Some cashiers regularly complain of this, but Cashier Mind and Body™ wonders whether this is not just pure fabrication.

Get Firmer Breasts!

Yes! For you ladies, as amazing as it sounds, the job of cashier has a big advantage for you! You carry a variety of heavy objects, and you rotate nearly 120 degrees with these items, which tones your pectorals. The result will be visible after only a few weeks. Your breasts will be firmer!

It's easy to compare yourself with women who aren't as lucky as you. A customer passes by? A new cashier arrives? Look at her chest area and then look at yours, which already has several months' work behind it. Can't you see a clear difference? Cashier Mind and Body™ has proved it: checkout girls have nice, firm chests. No more droopy boobs!

Small downside: there is a slight risk of straining your back, and this exercise is, of course, better suited to women. Some men might have to wear bras after a few months.

Develop Your Immune System

Before working on the register, did you get colds, sore throats, and the flu all the time? Permanent contact with customers will strengthen your immune system and make you resistant to all illnesses. What's more, by working near the freezers, automatic doors that are nearly always open, and air conditioning, you will become stronger in the long term.

Small downside: it appears that some employees will become more receptive to viruses because of prolonged contact with all these germs. A study is in progress, but there's no need to panic. Cashier Mind and Body™ suspects that some staff members have started this rumor as an excuse to blow their noses at the register in front of customers.

Learn How to Put Your Makeup On

Another bonus for the ladies: standing behind a register all day under fluorescent lights will cause your complexion to lose its natural sparkle. Not a problem—after a few months' work, you will have become an expert in applying foundation (not provided by the store) to put some sparkle back into your gray skin. And use your breaks to get some sun in the store's (noisy and polluted) parking lot. The reflection of rays on the cars will make you brown (or baked) in no time.

Give Your Brain a Break

Note, too, that with regard to the state and development of your brain, the automatic movements and phrases repeated a thousand times a day will allow your mind to take a break during your working day. You can engage your brain again when you leave the store. It's a good way of preserving your neurons for when you're old.

Small downside: some customers will confuse you with a houseplant or the village idiot. Let them; it makes them feel superior and they will be delighted to come back and do their shopping with you. You have won your first regular customers. Cashier Mind and Body™ is proud of you!

So, dear customers, the next time you do your shopping, take a look at the cashiers and observe the secret moves they use every day to create their dream bodies. Working on the register is even better than going to the gym! Bring on the water bottles and cat litter!

18

Where Hollywood Meets the Cereal Aisle

Perhaps you worry that your job behind the register will grow tedious, that after a few weeks of scanning cereal boxes and toilet paper, monotony will set in. No need for concern! Imagine that working at a supermarket is like going to the multiplex, and you've got the best seat (or lack thereof) in the house. Grab your box of microwavable popcorn (two for one with your club card), and let's go!

Movie 1: The Romantic Comedy

What happens when hilarious customer high jinks meet old-fashioned amore? Why, a romantic comedy, of course:

CASHIER
Hello!

CUSTOMER
Well, well. What's a nice girl like you doing in a supermarket like this?

CASHIER (*scanning the customer's hair gel and economy-size pack of paper towels*)
$19.68, please.

CUSTOMER (*scrounging around his pocket, hopefully for his wallet*)
So, tell me, did it hurt when you fell from heaven?

CASHIER (*avoiding eye contact at all costs*)
Do you need any cash back?

CUSTOMER (*twirling his debit card seductively in his hand*)
Yes, a quarter . . . so I can call my mother and tell her I just met the woman of my dreams.

Movie 2: The Action Sequence

Sometimes excitement occurs when you least expect it. Consider the following scene, based on a real-life experience, in which a customer has just escaped from a local mental hospital and has come to do some light shopping. Your manager, who has called the cops, has you open a special lane to keep the frenzied shopper occupied until they arrive.

CASHIER
Hello!

Customer lights a cigarette. Cashier ignores the no-smoking policy and scans the customer's fifteen bags of hot-dog buns.

CUSTOMER *(grabs a jelly doughnut and proceeds to "spank" the offensive pastry and scold it loudly)*
Bad doughnut! Very bad doughnut!

CASHIER *(ignoring the grape jelly flying in every direction)*
Do you have a club card?

Customer has moved on to the Boston cream doughnut, which is equally in need of discipline.

CUSTOMER 2 *(who has just entered the lane and is talking loudly on his cell phone)*
Excuse me, is this going to take all day? I have things to do.

CUSTOMER 1
Make the corn flakes stop staring at me!

CUSTOMER 2
There are others of us in line, you know.

CUSTOMER 1
Satan is in my cereal box!

CUSTOMER 2
Miss! I'm not getting any younger here.

CUSTOMER 1
Satan!

Fortunately, the police arrive and remove the insane—but aren't they all quirky in their own way?—customer before a fight breaks out, and you proceed to scan Customer 2's diet soda and hemorrhoid cream. There is no "job well done" or "thank you" from management. But that's OK: you, the unsung (and underpaid) hero, continue to fight the good fight, to protect and serve your customers. Under your careful watch, they will all live to shop another day.

Movie 3: The Police Drama

There's nothing like an undercover sting . . . except when you're the target. Imagine this: You're standing innocently at your register when a woman approaches with a six-pack of the cheapest beer in the store. She's got crow's feet around her eyes and is incongruously sporting a midriff-bearing T-shirt. The customer places her beer down on the conveyer belt and looks at you meaningfully.

CUSTOMER *(speaking loudly and deliberately; perhaps she thinks you're deaf)*

I'D . . . LIKE . . . TO . . . PURCHASE . . . THIS . . . BEER.

Your mind starts to wander. You think back to the supermarket lothario you met earlier that night, with the intriguing hair and flirtatious banter. Yes, perhaps some of his lines were a bit dusty with age, but he had nice eyes. And face it: it's been a while since you've been on a date. Maybe you were a bit hasty letting him go . . .

CUSTOMER
HELLO? I'D . . . LIKE . . . TO . . . PURCHASE . . . THIS . . . BEER.

CASHIER
Sure, sorry. That will be $6.19.

Suddenly an alarm sounds. Robby, the security guard (who still owes you five bucks from last night's poker game), rushes toward you, mysteriously dressed in a dark suit and sunglasses, swinging a pair of handcuffs. In a flash you realize what has happened. This was no ordinary customer, but a "tester" who works for the supermarket! She was testing to see if you would check her ID before selling her beer, and you failed miserably. What will happen now, you wonder in a panic. Jail?

Or worse—will you now be moved to aisle cleanup and stocking shelves? You look around desperately as you're escorted out the automatic doors.

So, as you can see, life in the supermarket is filled with drama, suspense, and intrigue. Why venture to the theater when all the supermarket's a stage, and the (sometimes unhinged) men and women merely players?

19

Thou Shalt Not Steal ✂

Supermarkets: veritable treasure troves but, unfortunately, everything has to be paid for. Sometimes, though, especially if your purse is empty—or you're a kleptomaniac—the temptation to steal is just too strong. It's only human. But if you don't want to get caught, dear customer, avoid the following ploys, which are all too well known by cashiers . . . or at least make sure that you perfect them.

The Smooth Talker

This ploy involves being very glib. The customer relates his life story and tells lots of jokes with extravagant gestures. This customer is a real clown—actually, a real magician. He hopes to distract the cashier's attention so that she won't notice that, underneath his coat, his stomach is strangely round.

Do you have the gift of gab? Give it a go, but be sure you have the necessary talent, or your next performance will be in front of a couple of police officers.

The Arguing Couple

While the cashier scans their items, a sudden, violent argument breaks out between husband and wife over why they have bought some products twice or the color of the toilet paper. The tension increases and they come to blows. The cashier doesn't know what to do and looks at the floor. The couple uses the opportunity to whisk through the checkout with a backpack full of groceries.

Forget this tactic. Most cashiers today love domestic disputes and won't miss a moment—unless you go so far as to tear each other's clothes off (but that technique might attract too much attention).

The Concealer

This customer puts a CD in a box of cereal, batteries inside packs of soda cans, etc. All products that could be used to "cover" others are well known by cashiers. You'll either need more imagination or need to come with a shopping bag with a false bottom. By the way, you can also forget the "Oh, I didn't see it!" excuse when the cashier discovers the booty.

The Outraged Customer

This customer is leaving with his groceries when the security alarm sounds. Immediately he cries, "It's a scandal! Unbelievable! You can't treat me like a thief. The alarm must be broken; this happened last time, too! I'm never coming back here." The customer is hoping to intimidate the cashier or the security guard so that no one will ask to see his purchases and will just let him through, worn down by his shouting. Even if you can be really frightening, forget this tactic. It has been used to death.

The Athlete

The athlete passes through the registers at the speed of light with a large item under his arm and takes everyone by surprise. You need to be extremely fit with a good knowledge of football tackles to avoid being flattened at the exit by the security guards.

The Bar Code Switcher

She will swap the bar code of the product she wants to buy for that of a cheaper product. Two drawbacks: First, the labels with the bar codes are very difficult—almost impossible—to remove, and they break easily. Second, you are unlikely to get away with it. The cashier will notice if a pan costs the same as a packet of salt. Don't take her for an idiot—it's an error that could be your undoing.

Out of Sight, Out of Mind

He waits in line like everyone else. The cashier thinks he's a normal customer who is quietly waiting his turn. But suddenly he leaves the line and makes a dash for the exit, his bag full of groceries under his arm. By the time the cashier can react and warn security, he is already home free. He counts on the passivity of the crowd and the weariness of the cashier. Nice try, but it won't work. This tactic requires the security guards also to be very tired, or else absent altogether. So you have to choose your time carefully and watch out for the security guards' break times. It might be a question of seconds.

I would also like to warn you about a final point: beware of other customers. Some are born to tell tales and won't hesitate to betray you to a cashier or to management. Honestly, I promise. So be careful when you steal in the aisles (and hiding a pan under your coat isn't very discreet anyway!).

Some useful advice, I hope. Good luck!

20

I'm the Boss!

Did you think that when you were on the register, you were alone at the helm dealing with the customers? Wrong. You're forgetting your boss—who has one eye looking out for you and one eye watching you. But who are these masterminds? What do they do? What is their day like? And what is the best way for you to manage your boss?

There are nearly as many managers as cashiers in supermarkets. Some will last a few days; others, years. Each will have his or her own method, goals, and principles.

The Efficient Boss

He has climbed the ladder, rung by rung, through hard work, and he certainly deserves his place. He fully understands the workings of the store and knows how to solve problems. He will be there to help if you have a problem.

Your register breaks down. You call your supervisor (naturally).

"My register is stuck."

"I'm on my way," the efficient boss replies immediately.

Three and a half seconds later, the door of the office opens and your supervisor emerges with a telephone in one hand and a screwdriver in the other. "Good morning!" he says with a big smile for the customer. "I'll take care of this little problem; it won't take a second."

Yes, managers like that do exist; I've actually met some!

The Eternally Dissatisfied Boss

Fear not—you will also meet some moody ones. They don't say hello. Want to try the same with your customers? (Oh, that's right; you can't—you're not a boss.)

You will also come across the moaners. When it comes to the sensitive issue of cashing out, these are the bosses who harass you, adding to your stress. And they don't see any more need to be helpful than they do to be nice.

"My register is stuck. I can't do anything."

"Again? Stupid registers! And stupid cashiers who don't look after their equipment," followed by an unintelligible grumble.

One of their minions will arrive a few minutes later to reboot the register. While you wait, you should tell the customer a few jokes to keep the bad vibes emanating from the telephone from reaching the customer.

The God Boss

This one thinks only about his career, his progress, and his personal goals. He forgets that staff members under his command still have rights. His weapon? Excessive communication. He writes hundreds of memos—on targets, turnover, and performance. He spells everything out for you. You'll almost feel involved in the running of the store—until your lovely boss reveals his predatory side.

If you say hello to the union representative and chat with him for a couple of minutes, you can be sure that thirty seconds later the boss will ask you if you have a problem with authority.

If you need to change your hours because of a personal appointment, you'd better beg someone to switch shifts with you unless you want to attract the rage of the God boss.

And if you are unlucky enough to contest a truly unfair decision by the boss, he will quickly call you to order with his unanswerable argument:

"I'm the boss!"

You've learned your lesson, I hope. Otherwise, punishment! No, not like at school where you take a note home for your parents and write out one hundred times, "I will never say no to my lovely boss again." It's another kettle of fish here. The good news will arrive with your schedule. You'll have horrible shifts (closing time every day—oh, joy) or a change of post. So you enjoy working at the customer-service desk? Well, apparently you don't smile enough, so you won't be going there.

The worst thing is that your boss will think that this punishment will be good for you. You think it will just cause more conflict. Obviously, you don't share his perspective on life (or his goals).

The Boss Who Wants Everyone to Smile

This one relies on mystery shoppers: customers who apparently report the good and especially the not-so-good behavior of the cashiers (I told you that some customers are born to tell tales). This boss is only trying to increase customer satisfaction. Her customers will be more satisfied if her cashiers smile more. Is this your boss? Lucky you, because she will try to do her best for her employees, she will always be in a good mood (or nearly always), and she might even lend you her support.

This is a rare species, so if you have one, don't let her go!

You should know, though, that your proven stupidity will force you systematically to appeal to your boss or his deputy for anything that is not explicitly part of your duties (you won't even be able to remove an item rung up in error on your own). And the surveillance cameras will always be on you. They will dissuade you from stealing a couple of pennies, catching a little nap, blowing your nose in a customer's bread, or picking your nose. In addition, thanks to the latest modern registers, your boss can follow your turnover in real time and "turn you off" when he feels like it.

So, do you see how work makes you free?

21

Your Conveyor Belt: Friend or Foe?

The conveyor belt—just another part of your register? Much more than that, actually. It is your friend! It is the first contact with customers and can prove to be a formidable ally. It has a few tricks up its sleeve to take revenge on those who treat you badly.

With the customer in a hurry who keeps throwing you looks of exasperation (it's your fault that the store is so busy) and who has emptied her cart like she empties her trash can, your conveyor belt (your friend) will jolt slightly. Splat, the box of eggs is on the floor and the bottle of wine falls and breaks and splashes on her nice beige pants. Hardly guaranteed to speed up the shopping process. And she'll have to wait for the maintenance crew to do its job. Poor thing (if you must smile, be discreet).

With the customer on the phone who completely ignores you when you help him pick up his change, which has fallen on the floor (not even a "thank you"), your friend the conveyor belt will eat the debit card he forgot to pick up (too busy talking on the phone). Your customer will have to wait at least twenty minutes to get it back. Oh, *now* he wants to talk to you!

With the child who won't stop crying all the time his mother waits in line (nearly fifteen minutes), who sticks his tongue out at you and throws his chocolate bar in your face, the belt will catch his fingers. Well, he shouldn't have tried to stop it. It's not a toy. He'll cry even more loudly now, but at least this time you know why.

With the customer who takes his sweet time, who doesn't care that the store closed ten minutes ago (do you recognize him?), and who loads his shopping on item by item, the conveyor belt will speed up, resulting in loud screeching noises. The noise will still be ringing in his ears when he has returned home.

But with the really nice customer who says "good morning" with a big smile and arranges her items from heaviest to lightest with the bar codes facing the scanner (wow!), the conveyor belt will be touched and let out a sweet purr. And everything will run smoothly.

Sometimes, however, the conveyor belt will let you down entirely—whether the customer is nice or not. It will change sides and support the customer. It will advance without stopping and unload all the items like a dump truck. It will be impossible to halt and will progress so zealously that your only recourse will be the emergency stop button (the big red button that works only every so often). The items will be damaged, and so will you. Don't forget that the customer will hold you entirely responsible (well, of course!). You can settle the score with these ungrateful conveyor belts at the end of the day with the spray cleaner (every small victory counts).

You might also come across one that, fed up with turning for years and years, will stop forever with a long and final rattle. A heartrending cry will indicate that your friend has left you, letting you down in front of a tidal wave of products and customers who think the belt has only malfunctioned. They will cry, "This always happens to me!" and push their items along with their hand, grousing and shouting at you because, of course, you are responsible for their misfortune. The conveyor belt will remain immobile, though. Immovable. Inert.

You think I'm exaggerating? Just wait. In the end, some days your solitude and powerlessness in the face of disagreeable customers will be so great that the slightest relief—even a malfunctioning or capricious conveyor belt—will be welcome.

So, in the evening, clean it with love, and when you arrive in the morning, give it a little pat. It will love you. Who knows—maybe one day it will eat a customer or the petulant head cashier.

22

How to Hide Your Fortune ✂

You will sometimes come across customers whose physique is the stuff of fantasy, and you will be surprised to find that you are imagining them naked and dreaming that you are massaging their feet (or possibly other parts of their anatomy). Then there will be others whom you'd rather not think about but who will be generous enough to let you enjoy a glimpse of some very appetizing parts of their body. They all have something in common: a terrible fear of being robbed, which makes them hide their cash against some warm, smelly part of their body. Average age: any (there are paranoid people everywhere).

When the time comes to pay, you will be lucky enough to get a close-up view of:

☛ Mrs. Jones's ample, flaccid bosom and her gray bra (it must have been white once) where she has hidden her cash. All is accompanied by a puff of eau de cologne or sherry (difficult to tell).

☛ Mr. Smith's scrawny foot and holey sock, where he hides his fifty-dollar bills. Drawback: an easily identifiable odor. Or maybe that's from the smelly cheese he bought.

☛ Mr. Thomas's bulbous stomach. His little arms always find it very difficult to reach underneath his sweater to his shirt, where he has hidden his money. And you can smell that he didn't have time to take a shower today (or yesterday, apparently).

☛ Mrs. Rogers, whom you can't see but can hear: "Wait, I don't have enough money; I'll just run to the bathroom." And when you see her a few minutes later—triumphant, with cash in hand— you refrain from imagining anything. You are just happy to take the money from her fingertips.

Yes, yes, I know, but you can't be fussy about where your money comes from—especially when you're a cashier.

23

I'm Paying

✂

Paying for groceries is an obligation that customers would avoid if they could. But, as you will have found out, customers make the cashier pay every day, each in his own way. Sometimes, you even start to ask yourself whether, perhaps, you are robbing the customers, given the seething looks and insults they throw at you. So you might be surprised to learn that some actually fight to pay. Yes, you read that right. They fight.

The scene below actually happened.

Two friends come to my register to pay for some ice cream and chips.

CASHIER
$7.99, please.

They both get their debit cards out at the same time.

FRIEND 1
Let me pay.

FRIEND 2
No, I should pay.

FRIEND 1
You paid for lunch yesterday.

FRIEND 2
Yes, but last week you did.

FRIEND 1
Yes, but you bought me the concert tickets.

FRIEND 2
That was a birthday present; it doesn't count.

FRIEND 1
You gave me a DVD, too.

FRIEND 2
Yes, but I'd promised to do that for ages.

FRIEND 1
I know, but I'd promised to get it for you.

FRIEND 2
It doesn't matter; last year you invited me over to
your house more often.

The cashier is starting to feel dizzy. But it's not over yet.
Friend 1 takes advantage of Friend 2's long reply to put her
card into the machine. Friend 2 grabs her hand, the card falls

out, and Friend 2 puts in her own. Friend 1 jiggles it and manages to remove it but doesn't have time to put her own back in. Friend 2 takes both her hands and stands in front of her. Friend 1 struggles violently and tries to reach the machine, which slides off its base, hits the register, and falls on the floor. But it's still not over. Friend 2 uses the confusion to put a twenty-dollar bill in the cashier's hand. Friend 1 is ready to tear her arm off to get it back.

CASHIER (*unsteadily*)
If you want to settle this, please do it outside. I don't want there to be blood.

They burst out laughing. And Friend 1 lets Friend 2 pay.

I think this little story reveals a quirk in our society. Paying is apparently the only real proof of friendship between two best friends. It's often the same in love: I pay, therefore I am.

Don't hesitate to remind your customers of this. They'll pay up more easily—you'll see.

24

Out of the Mouths of Babes ✂

A child's view of the world is full of insight, candor, poetry, and tenderness. Your heart will leap when you hear these innocent words:

LITTLE MICHAEL (*age seven, after watching your register closely*)
Where's your bed?

LITTLE NICHOLAS (*age nine*)
Can you give me money, too?
(Because he has seen you give his mother her change.)

LITTLE JULIA (*age six*)
Are you in prison?
(Because your register looks like a rabbit hutch.)

LITTLE ROSE (*age five*)
Mommy doesn't have any money to pay for her shopping. She can only give you a check.
(Because the previous customer paid in cash, and the little girl's mother had explained that she didn't have any change.)

All this is quite sweet and will make you smile. But when parents use you to scare their children, keep smiling politely (you have to) as you set them straight. When you hear a mother tell her child as she points her finger at you, "You see, darling, if you don't work hard at school, you'll become a cashier like the lady," there's nothing to stop you from explaining that it's not a profession for stupid people, that you'd rather do this than be unemployed, and that you actually have a good degree. (Five years in higher education? Really?) If you don't, you may find that children will see you as a failure.

Well, I have news for all those ignorant, self-righteous parents out there: it's been a long time since a degree guaranteed a dream job. Today's graduates sometimes have no choice but to do less skilled work. Dear parents, thank you for reducing our profession to a warning! Wake up: this is a new century.

25

MA, Checkout Operations ✂

People frequently assume that:

- ☞ Cashiers are less intelligent than professionals.
- ☞ Only high school students, lazy dropouts, and the disenfranchised elderly work the cash register.
- ☞ College graduates are overqualified for jobs in retail.
- ☞ Anyone working as a cashier who is over the age of eighteen must have no work ethic, no education, a drug problem, and/or cognitive deficits.

There's no proof of any of this. So why do we cashiers continue to put up with:

- ☞ customers treating us like automated machines?
- ☞ people talking to us like we're idiots?
- ☞ managers giving us no authority, even to cancel a transaction?
- ☞ parents using our profession to scare their children into doing their homework?
- ☞ our society still being eminently ageist?

Probably to shut up chronic moaners like me, retail has invented a very proper term to describe our function: "checkout operator." The debate is therefore closed and the problem solved, right? I dream of the day when all cashiers, customers, and managers are treated equally, whatever their age or level of education. We can all dream, can't we?

26

Chatty Customers: Your New Best Friends

Sometimes you will encounter the customer who comes to the store not just to replenish her milk and cheese supply, but to find a sympathetic soul (read: captive audience) to listen to her latest plight involving her no-good daughter-in-law or her latest medical diagnosis. These poor customers usually tend to be older women who are too proper and advanced in age to confess their troubles to a bartender, so they visit their local supermarket cashier, who is always happy to lend a friendly ear.

If you are lucky, you may encounter this scenario, most likely during your busiest shift:

CASHIER
Hello! Do you have a club card?

CUSTOMER
I did have a club card, but I lent it to my son, who of course gave it to my daughter-in-law, who can't organize anything. It's probably buried under a pile of dirty laundry in that place they call a home. Why she

needs a club card, I don't know. It's not like she ever cooks, if you know what I mean.

CASHIER (*shifting nervously as the line continues to grow behind the customer*)
That will be $99.50.

CUSTOMER
Everything is so expensive these days. Just yesterday my doctor told me I might need a hip replacement. Do you know how much that costs?

CASHIER (*trying to look as disinterested as possible*)
Paper or plastic?

CUSTOMER
And I can't understand one word of my Medicare statement. I'm convinced it's a government conspiracy. I would ask my son to explain it to me, but he's so busy with that wife of his. Did I tell you about her?

Cashier bangs her head repeatedly on her register.

So, as you can see, your register isn't just a place to earn a paycheck, but also a community gathering spot where, if you are lucky, you can make lifelong friends. But don't worry—if you fail to contain your enthusiasm and say something amiss to the chatty customer, you'll get to be the star of the tale she tells the *next* cashier.

27

"Your Register Is on a Break"

There will come a time when you have to tell a customer, "It's closed." And he will almost certainly reply, "But I've got only one item."

The first few times, you'll let yourself be convinced and scan the customer's sandwich, box of cereal, or low-energy light bulbs. But very quickly you will learn to refuse politely (since there will always be others behind complaining that they, too, have only one item). Because, yes, even cashiers have the right to take a break and relax for a few minutes.

So why is a break such a big deal? In your office, if you want to leave your computer to go to the bathroom, have a cup of coffee, or chat for five minutes with a colleague, you don't need to ask permission. But you do on the register. It's like being back in elementary school.

☛ Want to say hello to a colleague in an aisle at the other end of the store? No, not possible during your working hours.

☛ Need to run to the bathroom? Have you asked permission?

☛ Want a cup of coffee? Have you begged for it?
☛ Need a smoke? Are any cashiers available to
   cover you?

It's 1 p.m. and you're hungry, but you need to ask before you can take your lunch break. In retail (at the register, anyway), that's how it works. You were hired to work on the register, and you can't leave your post without permission. Is it frustrating that you're being treated like a child (especially having to ask to go to the bathroom!)? Get used to it.

Whether it's a little local shop or a big supermarket, the procedure for asking for the right to leave your register is the same. You will engage in this little question-and-answer game on the telephone:

CASHIER
Can I take my break?

SUPERVISOR (*Which response will you get? Take a guess.*)
❏ Yes.
❏ Someone will come and cover for you.
❏ We'll call you back; too many people are on their
   breaks at the moment.
❏ Wait a little while; there's a surge of customers
   at the checkout.

Sometimes when the supervisor tells you, "We'll call you back," he might actually forget. You'll call back forty-five minutes later (because you support the right of the other cashiers on the registers to take their breaks) and the answer may well be once again, "We'll call you when you can take your break." You'll be seething inside but won't be able to let that show in front of the customer who hasn't done anything wrong.

Another fake smile, and off you go again.

✱✱✱

There's another awkward moment for many cashiers when they have to ask permission to go to the bathroom.

Imagine the scene: The store is packed, and you have been squirming at your register for two hours, hoping that your need to go to the bathroom will inexplicably disappear because you don't want to bother anyone. Unfortunately, the need remains and, after a while, you have to ask to close your register while you relieve yourself. You pick up the phone and try to be discreet with regard to the customers—who don't need to know that your bladder is full—all the while continuing to scan packs of toilet paper and slices of ham.

After several attempts (the line is usually busy), someone finally answers.

CASHIER *(quietly)*
Can I leave my register for a second?

SUPERVISOR *(in an irritated tone that doesn't bode well)*
Why?

CASHIER
I need to go to the bathroom.

SUPERVISOR (*Choose the most likely response.*)
❏ Um, can you wait a bit?
❏ You can take a break in an hour.
❏ You went a couple of hours ago.
❏ But you only started your shift an hour ago!

CASHIER
But it's an emergency.

SUPERVISOR
Ummm . . . (or another muttering noise) someone
will come and cover for you.

In that case, all you can do is hope that your replacement
comes quickly!

In some stores, codes are put in place to allow you to make
a request more discreetly on the telephone because being able
to say "Code purple," "Can I have a 157," "The sun is shining,"
or "1945" is more cryptic. Really, not every customer wants to
be witness to your discomfort, and those who do—you won't
find their little smiles very amusing.

It can be difficult to relieve your bladder when you're a
cashier.

✳✳✳

Let's get back to the subject of "breaks." It's a good day today—you've asked to take your break, and your request has been granted. You'll even have time to go to the break room!

But what's it like, this place where all the store's employees meet during the day? This room represents the object of all desire for a cashier, where she can leave her work and customers for a short while. So, how nice is it?

Well, there are several kinds of break rooms. Kitchens have all the perks: table, chairs, fridge, fresh coffee, microwave. In big supermarkets, however, the room is designed differently. There is no fresh coffee for staff, but rather an automatic coffee machine (not free, obviously), machines with chocolate and sandwiches (they're not free, either), and, if you're lucky, a watercooler (that *is* free; just cross your fingers that there are some plastic cups left). There are a few tables and chairs, but avoid taking your break at the same time as everyone else because open seats are rare. Then there's the line to heat up your food in the only microwave (it's a luxury if there are two).

It's a convivial room where the only decoration is an information board (instructions for giving the Heimlich maneuver, messages from management, advertisements, etc.). In a corner are a few magazines to browse through—the same ones that were sitting there six months ago.

But there may be hope for some of you. I have been told (I would have loved to see it) that in other big supermarkets, there are armchairs and a television (no decorations, though, and the paint is peeling).

But apart from having some coffee and eating a sandwich, what happens in this room? That's easy: people chat! About everything and nothing, working conditions, relations with other employees and the bosses. Basically, it is a place to exchange information and set the world right. But look around first to check that there isn't a boss in sight or a manager who might overhear. You want to complain about people, but you don't necessarily want the people involved to hear you. Anyway, it all happens very quickly, because with only a ten-minute break for a four-hour shift (depending on your state's regulations or union rules), you don't really have the time to bitch and moan.

Let me set the scene (stopwatches at the ready):

Eight hours of work? Lucky you: you get a half-hour lunch break.

You clock out and go to the locker room to get some change to pay for your coffee/sandwich/chocolate bar: five minutes gone (the corridors are long, and you have to go upstairs).

You go to the bathroom and wash your hands: three minutes.

You go to the break room: two minutes.

Already ten minutes gone; you've got twenty minutes left.

To save time, you have gotten used to eating cold food to avoid waiting until the microwave is free (so you save two to five minutes), which means you have a good eighteen minutes to enjoy your break before rushing back to your register.

Once you're settled, you flick through an old magazine that has been lying on a table for a few weeks. You are beginning to know the articles by heart.

A colleague arrives.

The discussion begins: you talk about working hours, break times, your last customers ("Can you believe it? He changed the label of the chrome coffeemaker but he's a bit stupid. It's obviously worth more than three dollars!"). You talk about your families, your vacations ("Is the boss going to grant me my week off?"), plans for evenings out, and the lack of time you have to spend with your friends or children.

One eye is still on the clock. People laugh. Another colleague arrives, and already your eighteen minutes have almost run out. You swallow your coffee quickly (Did it burn? Too bad; you don't have time for small sips!), stuff down the last mouthful of sandwich, and have to clock in again quickly if you don't want to go over your break time and be scolded by the boss. You have two minutes left (barely time to go downstairs) before the end of your break.

You leave your colleagues and rush off. Your stomach is a bit heavy, you clock in and return to your register, and customers are already following you, ready to jump on you as soon as the lane opens.

Do your breaks feel too short? It's a good way to learn how to manage your time and make the most of every minute. A cashier must be punctual!

28

Do You Have 10 Items or Less?

Yippee! You have been put on the "10 items or less" lane. A quiet day, then. If I were you, I wouldn't get too excited. 10 = 10? Not at your register. Good luck!

$$10 = 20$$

CASHIER
Hello! Do you have 10 items or less?

CUSTOMER
Of course! (Number of items on the conveyor belt = 20.)

CASHIER
Could you please go to another register?

CUSTOMER
You're just lazy!

10 = 11

CASHIER
Hello! Do you have 10 items or less?

CUSTOMER
Um . . . 1, 2, 3 . . . 11. Is that OK?

CASHIER
11 isn't 10.

CUSTOMER
You're not going to make a big deal about 1 little extra item?

CASHIER
10 means 10. But if you want, you can pay separately or remove 1 item.

CUSTOMER
Damn it!

10 = Nobody

CASHIER
Hello! Do you have 10 items or less?

CUSTOMER
There's no one else here; you can take my cart!

CASHIER
Sorry, but this lane is reserved for customers with 10 items or less.

CUSTOMER
Damn it!

$$10 = 5 \times 10$$

CASHIER
Hello! Do you have 10 items or less?

CUSTOMER
I've got about 50 items, but I'll pay in five different transactions.

CASHIER
Very clever. I'd never have thought of that.

10 = Come On!

CASHIER
Hello! Do you have 10 items or less?

CUSTOMER
No, but I never stick to that rule. I work at Discounts R Us, and the cashiers there let me through all the time.

CASHIER
Yes, but this isn't Discounts R Us.

CUSTOMER
Come on!

Being taken for an idiot, insulted, having to argue all the time, getting involved in controversy, never giving in, being intransigent, etc. So does the "10 items or less" lane still tempt you? Didn't you say that you had the symptoms of an ulcer? This is just the place if you want to develop one.

29

Paper or Plastic:
The Hot Debate

Ah, paper or plastic. The perennial debate. If you're lucky, your store offers only one or the other. But if yours offers both options, be prepared to encounter strong opinions on the matter.

Most customers will happily accept whatever bag you give them or, given a choice, will select whatever they can reuse in some way at home. But you may encounter a customer here or there with some ardent views on the subject:

CASHIER
Paper or plastic?

CUSTOMER
Plastic? Really? In the twenty-first century? Are you aware that plastic bags are recycled at less than a third of the rate of paper bags? Do you know where your plastic bags end up? In a landfill. Or even worse, blowing through our streets, or choking marine life in the ocean. How can you possibly offer plastic?

CASHIER
So . . . I take it you want paper?

Or you may instead encounter a vocal plastic-bag enthusiast who also has some strong opinions to express:

CASHIER
Paper or plastic?

CUSTOMER
Paper? That's the most despicable thing I've ever heard!

Did you know that the production of a *single* paper bag consumes a *gallon* of water? Are you aware that there are people around the world with no water at all? What kind of store is this?

I have half a mind to call the EPA!

CASHIER
So . . . I take it you want plastic?

You'll notice that neither of these customers has brought his own reusable grocery bag, a new option in many stores. For a small price, these environmentally conscious shoppers can save the forests and spare the landfills (and, in some stores, even earn cash back toward their purchase). And, dear cashier, you have a foolproof way to silence these muckrakers as they climb upon their discount soapboxes.

> **CASHIER**
> Paper or plastic?

> **CUSTOMER**
> . . .

> **CASHIER**
> I completely agree.

> Would you like to purchase one of our environmentally friendly reusable grocery bags? You can bring it with you each time you shop and earn five cents back on your purchase.

> **CUSTOMER** (*staring at his feet and mumbling*)
> Err . . . no, thank you. My wife will never forgive me if I don't bring back some free bags to line the trash can with. Money doesn't grow on trees, you know.

Yet, for other customers, it's not the type of bag you use, but how you bag their products that creates a stir. Some customers want paper bags *inside* plastic ones. Others are quite particular about the placement of their eggs or bread (always on top to avoid "crushed bread syndrome," a dire condition that will send your customer directly to the customer-service desk). Then, of course, there is the looming threat of the ice-cream carton dampening everything around it (beware, greeting cards; danger abounds!).

Were you worried there would be no growth opportunities as a cashier? You couldn't be more wrong. There is always a new skill to master, a new danger to overcome, and a new (paper or plastic) foe to battle.

30

Can I See Some ID, Please?

You thought that asking for ID for certain purchases was a formality that everyone would accept. How naive! You will discover that, for some people, showing ID poses a problem: it forces them to both confront and reveal some unsavory or "private" aspects of their identity.

Yes, ID will give you intimate information about your customer. And maybe he doesn't want you to know his age (he looks much younger) or his address (he's paranoid), or he's nervous you'll figure out his astrological sign (you know how private Cancers can be). Or maybe he's afraid that you will see his ID photo (he had a lot of acne then). Even worse, maybe you'll discover that he's not quite old enough to purchase those wine coolers buried at the bottom of his cart. So don't be surprised if you hear this kind of thing:

"What are you, the FBI?"
(No, the CIA.)

"But I'm thirty!"
(You want me to take your word for it?)

"You're joking!"
(*And the customer leaves without his groceries.*)

"Really? No one's ever asked me for that before."
(*OK, I'm an idiot.*)

"No need; I know your boss!"
(*And my sister knows the Beatles!*)

To some people, asking for ID is a capital offense, and they will get really angry and insult you when you refuse to let them purchase their alcohol. Be ready to duck, because they might throw it at you (even when it's a rare bottle of Château d'Yquem wine). They're clearly above the law. Or on the run from the law, maybe. (Even if the individual pays with a credit card, the cashier doesn't get all those details, but her boss will.)

Others will show you an ID belonging to their friend or grandmother. The photo is a bit of a giveaway. Yup, those customers really thought everything through.

CUSTOMER
Well, what's the difference? Anyway, my friend was here just a couple of minutes ago.

CASHIER
Can't you ask her to come back?
(Bizarrely, you didn't see the friend.)

CUSTOMER *(getting agitated)*
She's gone, for God's sake!

And the customer leaves her groceries and rushes off.

In any case, never give in (even if you find the customer very attractive). If there's ever a problem, particularly with an overseas check, your management will be quick to tell you that you didn't do your duty as a cashier and make you pay. And you're in for even bigger trouble if you're discovered selling alcohol or cigarettes to a cunning minor. Be an incorruptible cashier! (Besides, you can laugh inside when you see Mr. Jones's face when he was twenty on his driver's license or that Mr. Smith was bald two years ago, when today that's visibly no longer the case.)

It's All About the (Fake) Benjamins

Depending on your store's policies, you may find yourself in the demanding role of counterfeit-money inspector. For example, you may be required to check all bills larger than twenty dollars for the correct watermark and security thread. Since this will involve holding the bill up to the light, it's difficult to perform this task without the customer noticing. While most customers will tolerate this activity with only a slight bit of eye-rolling, there will be the occasional customer who will take it quite personally when you attempt to investigate the hundred-dollar bill he is using to pay for his one-dollar chocolate bar. This customer will just have to be patient; as a cashier you are on the front lines of policing potential criminal activity.

This role of protecting your store from nefarious counterfeiters involves many weighty responsibilities. You must keep up to date on the latest techniques used by the Department of the Treasury to separate the real bills from the imposters (updates are posted in the break room, in case you run out of reading material during your ten-minute break). You must be prepared to act quickly should such a villain dare try to perpetrate this heinous crime in your lane (don't worry; fake money is only a fraction of 1 percent of the genuine currency in circulation).

But lest you grow cynical: not every customer paying with large bills is a suspect. Since counterfeit bills are such a rare phenomenon, there are perfectly viable reasons for a customer to pay for a ninety-nine-cent yogurt with a fifty-dollar bill. Perhaps the customer:

- ☛ just robbed a bank (hey, as long as the bills are real, it's not your problem)
- ☛ has a very small money clip that can only fit so many bills
- ☛ recently won the lottery (but still does all his own grocery shopping—what a gem!)
- ☛ needs smaller bills for an upcoming jaunt to a gentleman's club (probably the same customer who proudly displays his condoms on the conveyor belt. Not only is he a seducer of women—he's rich!)

Your responsibilities don't end with checking bills. You should also be prepared to spot fake coupons (yes, that seemingly benign Bargain Hunter may be secretly plotting to shave an extra fifty cents off her detergent).

On the bright side, if your career as a cashier doesn't work out, you are well prepared for a job in criminal investigation.

Bless You!

NOTICE TO STAFF *(following several complaints from customers):*

Cashiers, do you have a cold? Please stay at home. Even if your doctor can't give you a note because your cold is benign, stay at home anyway, you plague-stricken person! Why? Because you touch customers' items with your hands, which are covered in germs, and you might sneeze at any moment and "blow your nose on their bread!"

Do you have a cold because customers are forever sneezing and coughing all over you? So what? The customer is king. They have a right to give you their bugs, but they do not want yours.

Enjoy your time off.

The Management

r--¬
¦   ¦
¦   # $19.99, Please!   ✂ ¦
¦   ¦
L--

Beeeep!

CASHIER
$9.99, please.

The customer hands you a ten-dollar bill. You give him a penny in change and bless the inventors of such tricky prices:

- ☞ $9.99 instead of $10
- ☞ $19.99 instead of $20
- ☞ $99.99 instead of $100

"That's a good deal! Quick; let's buy it! Life is cheap!" say consumers.

You can also thank these inventors for all the wonderfully fulfilling moments you will have. Instead of spending ten minutes cashing out, you will spend fifteen because of all the pennies, nickels, and dimes you will have been given during the day. And your fingers will be covered in a thin layer of copper mixed with . . . dirt. More than fifty times a day, you will have to answer the following questions and respond to the following remarks:

CUSTOMER
$19.99? Couldn't you just say $20?

CASHIER
Well, no. My job is just to tell you the exact amount to pay.

CUSTOMER
Can't you round it up?

CASHIER
I'm not in charge; talk to the management.

CUSTOMER
Keep the change!

CASHIER
One penny; how kind! But we're not allowed to accept tips, however small and generous they are.

CUSTOMER
I'm fed up with all these little coins in my wallet.

CASHIER
Save them for charity.

CUSTOMER
I'm one penny short. Can't you let me off?

CASHIER
Sorry, I'd like to, but it's not possible.

Yes, it works both ways. But don't forget that "$19.99, please" takes nearly twice as long to say as "$20, please." At the end of the day, the time lost must represent about two or three fewer customers served by the cashier. If I ran a supermarket, I'd rethink this pricing strategy.

34

My Register, My Love

Did you think that once you were in the swing of things life on the register would be easy? That you and your register are one, your gestures are automatic, you no longer have to think, and you neither hope for anything nor fear anything? Be careful! Depending on the store at which you work, a terrible danger may await you: management could choose at any time to send you to the register at the gas station to cover for a colleague. Then, panic! You will be completely lost.

In order to prevent the shock from being too violent and to prepare you psychologically, here are the main tests that await you.

Test 1

A register that is completely different from the one you're used to. Customers who want to buy a gallon of camping gas, who come and complain because the gas pumps aren't working, who beep their horns like crazy people, who poison you with their exhaust fumes. Oh, and don't be overly polite—they hate that.

Customers 1—Cashier 0.

137

Test 2

Are you trembling? It's not over yet. You will observe moments straight out of disaster films:

> *Everything was quiet that day until the arrival of a young man at breakneck speed changed everything. He tore into the gas station at one hundred miles an hour, stopped at the pumps, and took down a fire extinguisher.*
>
> *"Hey; he's stealing it!"*
>
> *Incredulously, I jump up. He notices me. Stopping in his tracks, he points in a particular direction. I look over and notice with horror a parked car with its hood open and flames coming out of the engine right next to the gas containers (a perfect parking place).*
>
> *Panic! The only thing I can think to do at the time is to call security. By the time they arrive, the driver has contained the fire. And all the while customers continue to fill their gas tanks.*

Customers 2 — Cashier 0.

Test 3

Don't worry; you will also be witness to petty crime (theft, holdups, etc.) and violent arguments (two drivers grabbing and pushing each other because neither wants to give way to the gas pump).

Customers 3—Cashier 0.

Just a word on what to do when these things happen: don't give in to panic; call security right away. (If you are keeping score, do it discreetly.)

Test 4

Beg and plead not to be sent to the gas station the day before a holiday or a long weekend. You might not survive that ordeal. Between the pumps, the noise of the cars, the screaming children, and the insults of customers rushing to get out of town before the holiday traffic, the struggle will be particularly difficult.

Customers 4—Cashier 0.

Ah, yes, the life of a cashier is full of unexpected events and dangers. So, another piece of advice: don't rest on your laurels. Let *vigilance* be your watchword.

On the other hand, one advantage awaits you at the gas station: you will have your own personal bathroom (with a door) only a few feet from your register (including a toilet that leaks and smells). Isn't life great?

Customers 4—Cashier 1.

* * *

There are other reasons to celebrate your trip to the gas station. If you survive the experience, you will have lots of stories to tell your friends, and when you're back at your register in the store, you will think you're in paradise. The insults, fights, horns, and holdups will be nothing but far-off memories.

I advise you not to read the following, particularly if you have been feeling fragile recently, but it would be profoundly dishonest of me to stay silent about . . . the other disagreeable surprises that await you. When you become a cashier, you should understand that you risk having to work:

At the Customer Service Desk

This is not as complicated as you'd think. You just have to find a few good arguments to shut up customers who come to complain that one of your colleagues didn't want to double-bag their merchandise, that the music is too loud, that the prices are too expensive, that the meat counter is not properly labeled or stocked (there's no Virginia ham), that there are too many customers, etc. Nothing too complicated, you see. Of course, you will also need to master all the subtleties of refunds, exchanges, lottery tickets, and club cards. Child's play, really . . . after several weeks of effort and a smile for every challenge . . . if all goes well.

In the Office

The great privilege of this post is that you will have practically no contact with customers. Nice, huh? The disadvantages: answering the phone, having to count the money in the safe, using the computer to find the bar codes of items when the cashiers don't have them, preparing schedules, and knowing how to answer any question that comes your way in three seconds. Not for everyone, I know. Especially if the computer gets stuck, but that never happens—well, almost never.

✶✶✶

That's a fairly exhaustive summary of the dangers that lurk. Keep calm. And I should have said this at the outset: these posts will be occupied only by cashiers who are really motivated. Management uses only the best ones (the ones with degrees or who are regularly number one in items scanned or whatever criteria they use—it all depends on your manager).

However, there is another kind of promotion (generally short-lived). With a bit of luck and skill (that your store will be happy to use when the need arises), you can get yourself a proper job: you can work in the aisles to replace someone who's on leave for a few weeks or months (accident, maternity leave, long-term disability, etc.). You'll love that. You get to finally leave the register to do something else! But don't get complacent: when the person you are replacing comes back, there's little chance of keeping your new post.

These replacement positions rarely last for more than a few months (if you're looking to skyrocket up the corporate ladder, cashier is probably not the position for you). So when it's the turn of other cashiers to fill in for someone, you won't have any reason to be jealous. They won't be paid more than you and won't change status. "Cashier" will continue to be written on their paychecks. And if they look down on you a bit during the replacement period, once they're behind the register again, they will go back to being the cashiers they always were.

OK, you can breathe easy now. In the end it's more frightening than dangerous. But the gas station? Sorry, that threat is very real, even if you never ask for it.

By the way, have I mentioned the self-service lanes (more profitable than even the most badly paid cashiers) that might replace you altogether one day? We'll talk about that when you're feeling better.

35

Game Over

Have you been working for a few hours nonstop? Do you feel fatigue coming over you? Careful! You are soon going to experience the "Little Beep Moment," a great moment in your day. Let yourself go and embrace this surreal occurrence.

The store is very busy. Carts are bumping into one another in ever-greater numbers, the wheels grinding and creaking. All around you, harried customers come and go incessantly. The loudspeakers crackle out the latest special offers and the background music becomes insistent.

The ambient noise is getting more and more unbearable. Your maximum threshold has almost been reached. All that's needed is one more loud noise, and you'll be tipped into another dimension. It's the yelling of a child that does it. For about sixty seconds you exist in a parallel universe.

The noise, the conversations, the music—it all stops. Customers, colleagues, the entire supermarket disappears. Now, you hear nothing but the beeps of your register answering those of the neighboring register. Suddenly you feel like a match is on, as if a virtual tennis ball were going back and forth between you and your colleague. You're playing Pong!

After that furious game, it's on to Breakout, the famous Atari arcade game developed in the late 1970s. Your hands are the paddles, and the balls are the items that you have to send to the other side of the conveyor belt without them falling over or, worse, bouncing off other products. If that happens, an enemy ball might appear (if the customers agree to play). But, in general, the levels are quite easy! The only real problem is when the customers' groceries stack into a 3-D brick wall.

At the end of the level (the time of payment), the big monster invariably appears. To beat him, you have to be quick. Don't forget to shoot him with a club card inquiry and finish him off with a "good-bye-thank-you" accompanied by a glittering smile.

Take caution: some monsters have secret weapons like Unreadable Cards or Unreadable Checks.

✳✳✳

Sixty seconds later, the beeps and muffled background noise give way to the usual roar of the supermarket.

You have just experienced what I call the cashier's "Little Beep Moment." It generally occurs when you have passed your six thousandth beep of the day. Sometimes, however, you will leap into a game of Pac-Man, endlessly consuming the same little products—generally after your three thousandth "swallowed" item.

36

Did You Say "Bar Codes"?

Who said that your job as cashier was monotonous? Don't forget the customers. Thanks to them, the days follow from one to another but are never the same. Customers will never cease to surprise you.

Like the one who came to my register without any items. He handed me a list, on which I saw that he had scrupulously noted the twelve-figure bar codes of all the items he wanted to buy (about twenty of them). Here, I said to myself, is a customer ahead of his time. Did he hope that by the time I had scanned his bar codes, an employee would be outside in front of his car with his order ready? Or did he expect home delivery? Or had he applied the principle of "large items can be collected at customer service" to all items in the store, so as to be more practical?

I may never know. When I refused to scan them, he irritably replied, "I always do it like this!"

Really? Sorry, but I don't work in a cyber-supermarket. Give me the address and I'll apply, though. (Think about it: a piece of paper is much lighter than a case of beer!)

Just so you don't live your entire life behind the register without knowing, the numbers under the black bands on the bar codes represent a UPC, which stands for Universal Product Code. The standard UPC is twelve digits and includes a six-digit manufacturer's code, a five-digit product code, and a one-digit "check digit." There is a unique bar code for every kind of product. Now you'll never scan another bar code in the same way, right?

37

Strangely Sticky

One day you may be fortunate enough to come across this guy. He looks really nice. He says hello and even smiles. And he puts his shopping down on the conveyor belt properly.

Ten out of ten!

I scan his yogurt, case of beer, ham, cheese, and bag of chips . . . and feel something sticky.

"Strange," I say to myself. "No jam or honey coming up."

After putting the bag down, I look at my fingers and notice a small, indefinable substance. I look more closely, rubbing my fingers together. I still can't identify what it is. I stretch it; it's elastic and remains stuck to my finger. Then I get it: it's a booger! Yes, how nice of the customer to give his cashier such a gift. Would you like a packet of tissues with your chips?

I had a lot of trouble getting rid of it. It was really very sticky.

38

Drunk Customers

✂

Drunk customers will never fail to astonish you. They are never short of ideas or ridiculous arguments. Whether it's the one who asks you if you have a corkscrew to open the bottle of wine he has just bought. Or the one who falls head over heels in love with the first customer he sees, shouting sentimental drivel from across the store. Or the one who thinks he's Santa Claus and generously distributes the store's products to other customers.

Imagine watching a customer drink an entire six-pack of beer (well, maybe he's really thirsty and the soft-drink aisle is too far away). Beware of the beer aisle (what were you thinking, returning the six-pack of Stella a customer left at your register fifteen minutes earlier?), lest a drunkard fall in love with you and declare his passion with pauses for hiccups, releasing bad breath that could knock you over.

Remember the customer who was so drunk that you wondered how he found the supermarket alcohol aisle in the first place (a sixth sense, undoubtedly)? Then again, when inebriated, it's difficult to walk and avoid things that are suddenly in front of you: a shopping cart, a pack of

149

water bottles on the floor, a leaning tower of toilet-paper rolls (that is, before he tripped over them and they fell all over the floor).

Grab some popcorn—it's hard work watching people make fools of themselves.

39

There Will Be Blood!

Did you think that, despite the insults and the way people look through you as if you weren't there, your store would actually be a civilized place? Don't you believe it! When I tell you that working in a supermarket means seeing all sides of humanity, I really do mean all!

Screams. A chase through the supermarket. A security guard and a madman exchange blows. The first onlookers stop and take in the scene. The man calms down. The security guard holds him firmly by the arm. They move away. The guard is breaking out the handcuffs. People, more and more of them, surround the mayhem. But the madman hasn't given up. He has a captive audience now.

The fight takes a violent turn as the madman attempts to wrestle himself free. Fists, legs, and elbows are flying. Customers stand in a circle and watch the fight escalate. Men, women, children, bags, and shopping carts mingle and stare. Between blows, the guard radios for backup. It takes three security guards to overcome the madman.

The bloodier and more obscene, the better. Hey, look! Blood is pouring out of the security guard's nose. Wait until I tell everyone about this!

The other guards try to take the madman to a quieter place. The crowd follows. The guards move away again but manage to take only a few steps before the man flies into a rage once more.

Four men have a violent struggle. There are at least thirty spectators, but no one takes action. There are just as many employees open-mouthed in front of this spectacle. It's the same with accidents and fights in the street: everyone watches but no one reacts. The brawl ends with the arrival of the police, who take away the troublesome customer.

Once the show is over and the last curious people have left with their groceries (the final scenes of the brawl playing merrily in their heads), only the first security guard remains. He wipes away a trail of blood—the last vestiges of a fight in an improvised ring.

The moment of mayhem has passed—a moment when men allowed instinct to trump civility. And you remained behind your register—your protective barrier—unable to react.

40

```
┌ ─ ─ ─ ─ ─ ─ ─ ─ ─ ─ ─ ─ ─ ─ ─ ─ ─ ─ ─ ─ ┐
```
Idiots!
```
└ ─ ─ ─ ─ ─ ─ ─ ─ ─ ─ ─ ─ ─ ─ ─ ─ ─ ─ ─ ─ ┘
```

When you accepted the post of cashier, you thought that you wouldn't learn anything except the essentials of your wonderful job. How wrong you were! You are in a perfect position to witness the entire range of human stupidity—and you will be delighted to know that it is limitless. In fact, it's enough to make you foam at the mouth.

Saturday, 8:30 p.m.: you have scanned the items of 350 or 400 customers (a good day). They have mostly been pleasant, and some even very pleasant (they greeted you when they were on the phone). Your hearing is starting to return to normal. The announcer promoting the "special offers on beer" finally shut up a few minutes ago. Your conveyor belt is like new. You have cleaned it with love. Your trash can is closed properly. No pieces of paper or chips are lying around. The store is almost empty. All you have to do now is take your cash drawer proudly back to the office. You tell yourself that, for a Saturday, it could have been worse. To celebrate, you start to whistle your favorite song (or whichever one has been played twenty times through the loudspeakers that day). Then two men arrive at your register carrying three cases of beer.

CASHIER (*pleasantly*)
Sorry, but this register is closed. You'll have to go to the register over there. That one's free.

She points to an open register a few feet away.

FIRST MAN (*unpleasantly*)
Come on; you can take us. We've only got three cases.

CASHIER (*firm but internally scolding herself for so zealously cleaning her station*)
Sorry; it's closed.

FIRST MAN
I'll give you one dollar—then you can take my bottles!

CASHIER (*still firm but wishing a security guard would turn up at any second*)
No, thank you—it's closed.

SECOND MAN (*very unpleasantly*)
Come on! Cashiers are like whores! When you offer them money, they always say yes! Take our beer, you whore!

The cashier is now wishing she were Arnold Schwarzenegger so that she could (repeatedly!) knock their heads against her very clean register while telling them, "Enjoy your beer, halfwits!" You can always dream.

41

Can You Go to the Next Register, Please?

How can you annoy a customer legally?

It requires an elaborate scheme. You are about to open, but first you have to run to the restroom (with special permission, of course). Your colleague, two registers away, is just getting settled, and between the two of you stands an empty, closed register.

The customer (preferably in a bad mood) arrives at your colleague's register. She is far from ready (what a lazybones!) and sends him to you. He lets out a sigh. He doesn't see you (you are still making yourself look glamorous in the restroom) and thinks your register is the one just next door to your colleague's. He waits for you. Another sigh. You return (finally!), but he doesn't see you approaching from behind.

Two customers, who have been following you, line up at your register. At the same time, your colleague warns the customer (the one who's still waiting) that you are at the next station. Another sigh and he says, "She could have told me that she wasn't here!" Another sigh. He heads to your register, where a third customer has just arrived. Another sigh. You have started to scan the items of your first customer. Another sigh . . . and another, and another.

Your colleague indicates that she is open (sorry; her *register* is open), so you tell him, "My colleague has just opened. You can go to her register." The customer lets out yet another sigh and a stream of expletives, abandons his cart, and leaves, disgusted. Poor thing. Cashiers can be so disorganized!

We'll play again tomorrow; I promise.

42

Will It Scan or Not? The Six Steps for Getting Prices

When you got up on this Saturday morning, you decided that you wanted to be the best cashier of the day. This evening, your number (not your name—don't push it!) will be at the top of the office Items per Minute board. A nice challenge! (Though I must remind you that to encourage you, management will pay you not a single penny extra for this victory.)

You started an hour ago, and you are keeping up a very good pace. You decide to speed up a bit when suddenly, beeeeep! On your register screen you see "unknown product." Yes, you know what that means: the item in your hands won't scan. And if you don't know the price, you're stuck.

Don't panic.

Step 1

Enter the numbers on the bar code. Still nothing? That's normal—there was only a 1 percent chance that it would work (still, it was worth a try).

157

Take a deep breath.

Step 2

Call the office. Line busy? Bad luck. Wait and smile at your customer, who is starting to lose patience. Finally, someone answers!

CASHIER
The price for Super Softies extra-soft toilet paper, please; the code isn't going thr—

MANAGER (*interrupting*)
I'll send someone over.

Wait again (I know—what fun!), tell your customer (who is starting to turn red in the face) that someone will be there in a second, and tell those behind him to go to another register (if not, I warn you, you'll get sighs and shouts within thirty seconds).

On to Step 3 · · · a Good Five Minutes Later

The "runner" has arrived (finally, but hard to blame it on him when you know he has to handle a dozen registers all by himself). You immediately give him the toilet paper. The runner (a new employee) asks where to look. Oh, crap! You want to send your customer to help him, but you decide not to. He is crimson by now.

Quick · · · on to Step 4

Tell a few good jokes to your customer to make him relax and to make sure he stays (he might leave you with all of his groceries). Don't be afraid to use your secret weapon: "I have a minibar under my register. Can I get you a drink?" He smiles; it's working. The runner is back already with the price. Incredible! (You're not so unlucky after all!)

Quick · · · Step 5

Call the office to register the item, its bar code, and its price on the central computer. The computer has crashed! Don't lose your cool now; only a "few" seconds to wait. And smile; it's not your customer's fault.

Step 6 · · · Nine Minutes Later

Beeeep! OK, the Super Softies toilet-paper roll has gone through.

So, you lost fifteen minutes and nine customers? Your place as number one is severely compromised. Never mind—you'll win next Saturday. Or you can make up time during your break.

Oh, goody! A Bargain Hunter has come to your register. It's definitely not your lucky day.

43

Roll Up, Roll Up: It's Sale Time

What I'm about to describe doesn't apply to every store. But since it's a pinnacle to which every diligent cashier can aspire, I would be remiss if I didn't offer you some perspective. If you work at a certain type of store—one that offers everything from frozen waffles to curling irons to big-screen TVs—you may encounter a unique phenomenon: the storewide sale.

The first day of a sale is an important event in the life of the organized consumer, who wouldn't miss it for anything. For the cashier, it is a new opportunity to delight in being at work and not on vacation on a desert island.

8:25 a.m.

The Opening Time couples, the morning crazies, the Bargain Hunters, and all the rest can be counted in their dozens. Never before will you have felt so strongly that war has been declared or, if you watch too many horror films, that zombies are attacking.

There won't be enough sale items to go around, so have no pity! Today, there are no scruples about shooting people seething looks, pushing and walking over one another without apology (don't leave your feet lying around all over the place, then!), being rude to one another (me first!), growling (is there a dog in here?), using carts like assault tanks—and good for you if you run over someone's foot (fewer competitors).

8:55 a.m.

You arrive at your register and swallow a yawn. You anxiously observe these dogged customers and prepare yourself psychologically for their relentless consumerism. It's going to be a busy day.

9 a.m.

The wild animals are let loose. May the best (most aggressive) win! Everyone heads for the technology aisle to get a good deal on a flat-screen TV. The people who came the day before to do some research are the first ones there.

Too heavy?

"Never mind. Sit on it, honey, while I go and pay for it. And bite or hit anyone who tries to take it!"

The DVD players are also going like hotcakes.

"Fifty dollars? A bargain! I'll take the last three."

"They don't have the remote control. You can't navigate through the menus of your DVDs without it."

"Never mind; a bargain is a bargain."

The clothing aisle, so lovingly organized by the employees before opening time, has become a real battleground in barely a quarter of an hour. Has a customer found the very dress she was looking for? She has grabbed it out of the hands of another girl who had just taken it off its hanger, knocking over a pile of sweaters in the process. Never mind—it is the very dress she was looking for. She beams a winner's smile and continues her search in the aisle. But suddenly, what has she seen just over there? The actual very dress she was looking for. What should she do? Drop the first one on the floor like an old cloth. The sales assistants can pick it up. That's what they're paid for. And she grabs the actual, only dress she ever wanted. But wait—is it way too small?

"Never mind. I'll go on a diet tomorrow."

Farther down the aisle, a customer has grabbed the woolen sock of his dreams, green with nice sprawling octopuses. Is the other one missing?

"Never mind. I'll upend the box to find it. Too bad if most of it goes on the floor. It will be easier for other customers to find what they want. Are people walking all over the socks? Who cares?"

9:10 a.m.

Over to you, dear cashier. It's an emotional moment: the first compulsive shoppers at the register. You will be surprised (even if nothing surprises you now) at the number of items sold by your store, items of whose existence you were not even aware (even though you've been working there for several years). It's a parade of unsold, unsalable, useless items. The waltz of the sales beeeep begins.

✳✳✳

Sometimes, a little lucidity (what am I actually going to use that for?) or guilty conscience (I'm already two thousand dollars in debt) or both will make customers abandon some of their great bargains at the last minute. So don't grumble if you find thermometers in the shape of bowling pins, solar alarm clocks, enormous cow-shaped slippers (with udders), granny panties, and shovels without handles in the chewing-gum display at the end of your checkout station. After your day's work, put them back in their aisles. It's a chance to see some new scenery after a whole day of standing at your register.

More than any other day, you will feel that you have become a garbage collector. Most of your customers will confuse your conveyor belt with a trash can and literally upend their shopping cart or basket. It's your job to take each item and sort through the mountain of bargains as

quickly as possible. Few customers bother with politeness—
too much of an effort. Luckily, you might be able to count
on your friend, the conveyor belt. Its jolts will make the pile
of garden gnomes, flowerpot holders, and planting trays fall
over and will easily swallow a few little pairs of underwear
and some T-shirt sleeves (damn, it's all ripped and it was the
last one, too).

You are well trained, but be prepared to see the same
scenes over and over again throughout the day:

CUSTOMER
Is that the sale price? I think it's a bit expensive!

CASHIER
Yes. I check each time that you have been given the
discount.

CUSTOMER
The price isn't on it, but it was one dollar.

CASHIER
I'll call to check.

CUSTOMER
If you must! But you're making me late.

An aisle assistant arrives with the actual price: fifteen
dollars.

CUSTOMER
Really? That much? That's not what I saw. I don't want it.

You will also have to call your supervisor (with a smile and in good humor) at least twenty times to cancel purchases. Some customers will have been a bit too quick to believe that the sale items won't actually cost them anything. Apart from misers, it's not the wealthiest people who come that day. Wealthy people don't need to shop during a sale. It's those on low and middle incomes who come to exact their revenge on the normally high prices and to prove that they, too, have the right to consume. A sale is a good way of making people who don't actually have any money spend it anyway.

The first day of a sale is an ideal opportunity to get a good look at the personality of the twenty-first-century consumer. It is an exceptional day that any cashier worthy of the name must experience at least once in her life (and more, if you enjoy it).

Have you missed your store's most recent sale? Don't worry! There are still special offers, stock clearances, and plenty of other ways to extract money from the unsuspecting customer. The year will be full of bargains!

44

The Weekend Show

Do you still want some excitement? Have you been hoping to show the world that a cashier can still be her own person, or nearly? With some self-sacrifice and a bit of luck, you could experience this kind of situation.

It's Saturday afternoon, it's raining, and there are lots of people hanging around the store. A woman arrives with two giant packs of diapers and hands me a coupon. "Don't forget to double this," she says. I look at the coupon and let out a sigh (internally, of course). I can see already where this is going. I have to tell her, "I'm sorry, but we're no longer doubling coupons." I point to the notice on the counter indicating the new policy. "See; it says so there."

"They always double coupons for me here," she retorts.

Having experienced this kind of misunderstanding before (it happens a lot), and in order to calm things down quickly, I phone the office to ask for confirmation. The customer can then see that I'm not talking nonsense (after all, I'm just a cashier).

So I call the office and ask, "You can't double a coupon anymore, can you?"

"No, you can't," comes the reply.

I hang up the phone and turn to the customer, repeating (yes, like a parrot) that no, you can't double a coupon anymore.

"Call your supervisor. I want to see her."

"Of course. I'll ask her to come."

I pick up the phone again. "It's me again. Could you come and explain to the customer why we can't double her coupon?"

At the end of the line, I hear an apologetic voice: "No, not right now. I'm on my own here. Besides, Andy is already sorting out a problem at the checkout. You'll have to deal with it."

"Oh . . . I'll see what I can do."

I hang up and turn to the customer, attempting to smile.

"Sorry, but my supervisor is busy with a customer. She can't come and talk to you right now."

The customer is very red. She starts shouting (so that everyone can enjoy the situation; how generous of her) and gesticulating. Although I try to remain unruffled, I also end up raising my voice because, by now, I've had enough.

Suddenly we are in a nice argument. She shouts. So do I. She yells. Customers covertly approach so they don't miss anything. A show—how exciting! Well, it's not every day that you hear a cashier and a customer arguing at full pitch!

Our "discussion" is doomed to failure, though, since neither of us will give in. After several tense minutes, I notice a supervisor out of the corner of my eye. What luck! Given the noise, he must have heard. He'll definitely come over and calm things down. But my hope is short-lived. He acts as if nothing has happened and turns to walk down the pet-food aisle.

The customer finally gets out her debit card. With an abrupt gesture, she flings it at me. It falls on the floor. That makes me even more annoyed, but I pick up her card, give it to her, and say, calmly, "Ma'am, I refuse to serve you. You've gone too far and I won't be treated like that!"

The argument ends abruptly. The customer apologizes, pays for her diapers, and leaves.

Ten minutes later, one of the girls from the office finally arrives. She has come to see whether I have been able to handle the argument. I describe the brawl and she tells me, "Go and take your break. Someone will replace you."

The moral of the story? A few days later, the rules change. The store now doubles coupons again. OK, it's not exactly a moral, but why should there be one?

45

The Big Christmas Rush

Ah, Christmas! A period of festivity and sharing? Frankly, for those of you who are lucky enough to work in supermarkets that stock a variety of seasonal nonfood items, December 25 involves exactly the same stress as the first day of a sale. It's all about quick execution, increased scanning, big crowds, grumbling customers, empty aisles, compulsive shopping, even more impatience than usual . . . Welcome to the spirit of Christmas! I know; it's horrible, but if you really want to enjoy the season to be jolly, avoid this job.

The morning of December 24: the same old story. War has just broken out and the zombies are attacking. Customers are buzzing like flies in front of the store doors (which open at 8:30 instead of 9 a.m.).

With the same dread of missing out, they stampede the fish/butcher/deli/bakery counters. They're stocking up for the big blowout tomorrow. "It's a shame we can't serve ourselves. We'd have the turkey, sausages, smoked salmon, ham, and pie in the cart already and we wouldn't have to yell at the idiot who pushed in front!"

From 9:15 a.m. onward, the same generalized chaos reigns in the aisles as at sale time. This time, it's because some customers can't understand why all the garland and colored lights might be out of stock on Christmas Eve and kick up a fuss (thirty-six of them simultaneously). Then there are those who arrive three minutes before closing and are still attacking the greeting-card aisle, colored envelopes flying in every direction, when the lights go out (darkness isn't great for reading "humorous" punch lines about Santa breaking wind in the chimney or maudlin poetry expressing how this Christmas you will "treasure the moments with the ones you love / while celebrating family and the elusive turtle dove").

And of course, at the registers you find the same cordiality and politeness as normal, but what's worse is that the customers are increasingly exhausted and broke from buying presents all day, and they still have several names to cross off their lists. You can read in their furious glances: "You expect me to pay an arm and a leg, and you want a thank-you as well?" and/or "You're not the one who has to cook this turkey, so hurry up, you stupid cashier."

But don't forget to keep smiling sincerely, even when they shout at you for the fiftieth time that day because you can't double their coupons or gift-wrap their boxes of crackers. "Your hideous brown bags are not very Christmassy!"

You must wish them "happy holidays" as you give them your nicest smile. And you will have to repeat at least 350 times, about five times more than normal, "Yes, I check each time that you have received the discount."

Actually, the comparison between Christmas and a store-wide sale is not accurate. The decorations (multicolored tinsel and plastic Christmas trees) are quite different. You might be wearing a Santa hat on December 24. For a sale, you might be wearing a goblin hat. In both cases, though, you will look ridiculous (and your stylish uniform won't help).

Another important difference to bear in mind is that, on Christmas Eve, your store will close at 7 p.m. instead of 10 p.m. Yes, but you can be sure that you will be just as tired and at the end of your rope.

When the doors finally close and you think that you can breathe again, don't be surprised to see a frustrated consumer getting heated and yelling, "Let me in! I have to buy a turkey!"

"We're closed, ma'am," the security guard replies.

"What? But that's not possible. I can't go home without a turkey!"

"We're closed, ma'am," he will repeat several times.

You are allowed to laugh (inside). If a chuckle slips out, you can pretend it was nervous laughter.

46

Countdown

Saturday, January 3: my last day. No, it's not a dream!

All the familiar gestures and words I've repeated tens of thousands of times—today will be the last time. I can't believe it! I'd like to sit down to think about it but . . . I have to work. ("Just because it's your last day doesn't mean you're being paid to do nothing!")

I arrive at the office and say hello, as I do every day (they actually answer this morning). It's the last time I will look at the board to find out my hours and which registers I'll be working on: register twelve until 3 p.m., register thirteen until 9 p.m.— oh, joy, next to the freezers all day! And I forgot my scarf!

As usual, I glance at my cash drawer and check whether I have enough coin rolls for the day. Yet again, I ask for one-dollar and five-dollar bills. I take a few sheets of paper towels (just in case a bag of chips breaks, a booger gets stuck to my fingers, a customer needs to blow his nose after sneezing on me, or I encounter another of life's pleasures) and leave the office.

I have only a few hours left working for this company. I won't feel the same about the customers I meet today. Do I have regrets? I wouldn't go that far.

* * *

11 a.m.: clocking-in time. Immediately I hear, "Are you open?"

For the first time, I don't answer (I don't care!). The customers (my last three hundred!) parade past, one after the other. Among them are some of my favorites: the customer on the phone, Mr. Smith with his holey sock and his smelly foot, the Bargain Hunters, the customer with his embarrassing toilet-paper rolls. Some very nice ones, too—no, not the customer on the phone who remembers to say hello, but ones who have read my blog, *Cassiere No Futur*, who wish me luck and promise to treat cashiers like human beings from now on. Hooray! That's a great leaving present (so I haven't wasted my time).

8:45 p.m.: announcement that the store is about to close. Already? The day has gone really quickly. It's all the emotion, I guess.

8:55 p.m.: my last customer.

"Where are the restrooms?" It's always nice to end with a classic.

I glance at the aisles to check that the Closing Time couple isn't nearby. No—what a shame! I would have treated them like kings this time. Never again would they have come to do their shopping at 8:55 p.m.!

The day is over. I clean my conveyor belt with particular care ("I'm going to miss you, you know. Thanks for helping me so much.") and the rest of my checkout station. It is all so automatic that I almost forget why I'm doing it. This evening, though, I know that it's for the colleague who will take my place tomorrow. I wonder who will replace me on this register? You don't normally think about that. Why should you?

Last check. Last look from this side of the register. Everything is in order; nothing is lying around. With my cash drawer under my arm, I walk down the line of registers one final time to the office. The white tiles seem to continue endlessly in front of me. My feet are taking the same path that they have followed almost every day for the last few years, though. It is difficult to tell myself that the next time I come here, I will just be a customer. I slow down. I want to keep a bit of my soul here.

The doors close. The blinding white fluorescent lights are turned off and I am left in the shadows. My footsteps resonate in the great empty store. A solitary *beeeep!* can still be heard like a good-bye from the registers I used all these years. But it's time to go to the office and cash out for the last time.

The amount is correct! It's strange to think it's the last time I'll handle all those coins and bills. I return the money to my cash drawer, and I close it for the final time. I give it to my colleagues in the office. The label with my number will soon be taken off and given to the person who will replace me.

Who will, then, become just a faceless number.

Cashiers come and go, and one looks much like the other . . . or do they?

✳✳✳

A little glass of champagne? Orange juice? Some good-bye cookies at least? Dream on. You were a cashier, remember—not a lawyer! My colleagues hug me. It's a good thing they're witness to this moment.

I clock out one last time (well, I hope so!): 9:15 p.m., right on time. Ah, that capricious machine that made me enter my card over and over again. This time, I win! Someone else will be using this card tomorrow.

I think that the registers will haunt me for a long time. The lights, the background noise, the familiar faces of all the customers I met over the years, all the colleagues I worked with. All that is over for me today. Eight years behind the register (amazing!). I leave with a big (recyclable) shopping bag full of memories and beeeep, beeeep, beeeep . . .

So, do you still want to be a cashier? Is it still your dream job? No? I didn't think so! But do you have a choice? No? Good luck, anyway. If it's really terrible, do what I did and write a book. Who knows—maybe it will be sold in supermarkets for $6.99. Keep the change.

Acknowledgments

Thank you to all the colleagues who helped and supported me and made me laugh over those eight years on the register, particularly those who have become real friends.

Thank you to the first readers of my blog who gave me a reason to keep going and put it down on paper.

Thank you to Iris and François, who helped me so much with my writing.

Special thanks to Liliane, my eagle-eyed proofreader, for her excellent advice.

Thanks to my family, who are always supportive and who pushed me to fulfill my ambitions.

Finally, above all, thank you to Richard, my husband, for always being there.

About the Author

Anna Sam

Anna Sam was born in 1979 in Rennes, France, where she still lives with her husband and two dogs. Originally published as *Les tribulations d'une caissière*, *Checkout Girl* has since been published in twenty-one countries, selling over 350,000 copies worldwide. She has since written a second book—also set in the supermarket—and now dedicates herself to the cause of employee advocacy in her new role as supermarket consultant.

Morag Young

Morag Young studied French and Italian at the University of Leeds and subsequently worked for the European Parliament in Brussels and the Council of Europe in Strasbourg. She lives in Kent, England, and works as a translator.